Urban Dreams

Stories of Hope, Resilience, and Character

Edited by
Maurice J. Elias
Gina Ogburn-Thompson
Claudine Lewis
Deborah I. Neft

Hamilton Books
A member of
The Rowman & Littlefield Publishing Group
Lanham • *Boulder* • *New York* • *Toronto* • *Oxford*

Copyright © 2008 by
Hamilton Books
4501 Forbes Boulevard
Suite 200
Lanham, Maryland 20706
Hamilton Books Acquisitions Department (301) 459-3366

Estover Road
Plymouth PL6 7PY
United Kingdom

Library of Congress Control Number: 2007934246
ISBN-13: 978-0-7618-3843-2 (paperback : alk. paper)
ISBN-10: 0-7618-3843-0 (paperback : alk. paper)

This book is dedicated to Monique Cooper-Benjamin. Monique was a student in the Plainfield Public Schools who fought illness with courage, treated others with respect, and changed the lives of many with her strength, hope, and goodness. She passed away before entering high school, but her memory serves as an inspiration to those who feel that they cannot cope with their circumstances or those who feel they should abandon civility and empathy for hatred or despair. Her 5th and 8th grade *Laws of Life* essays are included in this book, as is a *Law of Life* essay by her remarkable mother, Judith.

Table of Contents

Editors' Introduction

Did you dream about the future when you were growing up? Virtually every child does. This includes youth growing up in urban America. Although movies like "Crash," the pages of our newspapers, and pictures on our televisions can make one certain that such dreams are going to be tarnished by the harsh realities of poverty, injustice, and racial prejudice, we believe otherwise.

Many children in elementary, middle, and high school wake up and look at the world each day believing that their lives are going to be different from what the headlines show and many predict for them. Along the way, they develop *Laws of Life*: strong values and principles that guide them in everyday decision and actions. Even at relatively young ages, children absorb these life lessons from their experiences and those around them. They use their *Laws of Life* as like beacons in a fog, as airplanes use navigation systems in heavy rains and clouds, and boats use a gyrocompass, the modern North Star, when seas are in turmoil. Yes, the difficult conditions of life claim some victims. Some children do not develop clear *Laws of Life*, and others develop *Laws of Life* fueled by hatred and revenge. But this does not happen as often as one would expect. Why? As urban educators, community residents, and parents, we believe that children can be sustained by their positive *Laws of Life* when these are nurtured and encouraged by even one or two caring adults around them.

Urban Dreams: Stories of Hope, Resilience, and Character is a collection of essays written by students in Plainfield, an urban community in New Jersey. This community has about 80% ethnic minority residents. Only one in five have a college degree of any kind, and almost 20% live below the poverty line (as compared to 9% statewide). One in four households has only a female adult and children under 18 years of age. The unemployment rate in this community is 150% of the national average, and the violent crime risk index is more than double the national norm. The children in this community are clearly at a disadvantage when compared to others in their state and across the nation, but not much more so than other youth who grow up in other urban centers where opportunities are also outnumbered by adversity. Efforts at diminishing this adversity certainly must not cease. Such children and teens do not emerge unscathed from their experiences, yet they have not lost all hope for the future. There is more to the character of these youth than many typically expect. Along the way, caring individuals have helped them to develop ways of looking at their lives and the world around them that causes despair to take a back seat to optimism. This book gives expression to these childrens' *Laws of Life* and shows how their spirit has been sustained despite the presence of so much around them that could be seriously destructive.

The essays were written when all schools in the district adopted and modified an inspiring idea from Sir John Templeton, the noted financier and social philanthropist, namely, that writing about and sharing one's *Laws of Life* can be a source of positive guidance for youth growing up in troubled circumstances. He began to encourage the writing of such essays as part of his *Laws of Life* Essay Contest. It started in rural Tennessee, his home, and grew in popularity to the point where it has now been adopted world-wide. Essays are being written in approximately 34 countries, from Argentina and Australia to Colombia, China, Ghana, India, Morocco, Russia, Sri Lanka and Uganda.

Typically, essays from the United States have been written by high school students. They have rarely come from urban communities with schools that are virtually all African-American and Latino, academically low-performing and beset by an array of social and socio-economic challenges. In 2001, Plainfield changed this statistic by becoming the first school district in New Jersey, and one of the first urban districts nationally, to embark on the *Laws of Life* journey. The district made a commitment to systematically help children to put into writing and share with classmates, family members, and the community the positive ways in which they are trying to live their lives.

Educators and parents in Plainfield agreed that waiting until high school did not make sense. Too many children dropped out, left the community, or had accumulated demoralizing experiences that had thoroughly jaded them and made it impossible for them to benefit from anything the school might offer. So, the *Laws of Life* project began instead in 5th Grade, the year before students made the transition from elementary to middle school. The process (described in "About This Book" and in the *Appendix for Educators*) is designed to create a dialogue, both inner and outer, that generates many new conversations between children, classmates, parents and guardians, educators, and community residents about character and the *Laws of Life* by which one lives. Inner dialogue is the process of reflection that allows children to make explicit to themselves the *Laws of Life* that are often operating in the background of their lives. The process of writing essays and talking about the deeply personal content gives children a sense of hopefulness: They learn that others have similar ideas and aspirations. Research has shown that this kind of elaboration of one's values is essential to putting them into action. Becoming conscious of and affirming our key life principles often makes it easier for us to draw on them in difficult situations. When one is struggling in water, knowing which of the many lifelines is truly a strong one is an essential survival skill.

WHY IS STORYTELLING SO IMPORTANT?

"Human beings are storytellers by nature. In a multitude of guises, as folktale, legend, myth, fairy tale, history, epic, opera, motion picture, television situation comedy, novel, biography, joke, and personal anecdote, the story appears in every known human culture" (Dan McAdams, *The Redemptive Self: Stories Americans Live By*, New York: Oxford University Press, p. 76). It is worth reflecting on why this is so, and over the years, many people have done so. Psychologist Jerome Bruner believes that human beings are "wired" to be storytellers and that stories are the way we organize our understanding of life, both the lives of those around us, and our own lives. As children learn more about themselves and bring a more informed and empathic perspective to the world around them, their stories become deeper and more insightful as regards motivations (both their own and those of others), and the children also become more capable of projecting their stories into the future, including their own, personal ones.

As they begin to look at their own lives and put their varied experiences into narrative form, children also start to speculate about their future. Many come to realize that their stories do not have to end as they began. They see that they can find the good in their stories and in their own actions as well as those of supportive people in their lives, and can therefore create a hopeful story, even an empowering one, one which reveals their resilience. And, when children share their stories with peers, they are all more likely to realize that the endings of their stories remain to be created and can be "surprises" to those who might tend to view them pessimistically. Of course, when adults see and hear children's stories, they, too, get a chance to revise their view of the narrative direction of the childrens' lives. They begin to see different story lines, less obviously stereotyped, or "type cast."

Indeed, we are using our long and extensive experience in Plainfield to illustrate a more general reality obvious to some but perhaps not to many: Urban youth, so often the object of remediation, programmatic interventions, and sub-jected to the pedagogy of poverty learn the way others do, via hope and inspira-tion. Further, their life circumstances, intense challenges, etc., make them no less capable of progress and accomplishment than are other youngsters. Still, as any reader can see, their road is more difficult. Parents of more advantaged children should give some earnest thought to the question of how theirs would fare under similar circumstances. At the same time, these children and their caregivers are by no means helpless or hapless victims of their circumstances. Despite extraor-dinary obstacles and difficulties, their moral compass is not only intact but bet-ter focused on life principles than many others of their same age, perhaps as a result of writing these essays and having the conversations that flowed from them in their classrooms, homes, and community.

Parents of disadvantaged children, policy makers, educators, and others should also not give in to despair or hopelessness. Those entrusted with the care and nurturance of children should ask whether what is often a myopic focus on academic scores is really in the best interest of children, or whether it is driven by adults' concerns with accountability and success. To "leave no child behind" is not an adequate goal; there is limited satisfaction in being brought to the back of the pack. Rather, we should aim to relentlessly seek the advancement of all children. In so doing, we affirm our commitment to prepare them for the tests of life, and not for a life of academic tests. The essayists in *Urban Dreams* de-sire and deserve this from the adults who are charged with responsibility for their care and development. While we should continue to try to improve the cir-cumstances that beset them and the inequalities that Jonathan Kozol and others have written about so passionately, we need not wait to help children give ex-pression to their aspirations about how to live a good life despite these circum-stances. In these essays, one also finds universal themes not limited to urban youth, such as how to deal with the loss of loved ones, how to derive inspira-tion from parents, grandparents, siblings, and even caring strangers, and thoughts on the power of faith. Perhaps most importantly, these essays reveal the resilience of youth when they are in positive, caring relationships.

The essays that comprise this book are the encapsulated stories of their au-thors, young writers who were given a chance to reflect on their own lives and those of their peers. While their stories often begin with great difficulty, most soon depart from the expected script. *Urban Dreams: Stories of Hope, Re-silience, and Character* is designed to show the world what is in the hearts of the youths that too many people have discounted, youngsters that too many view with pity and consign to hopelessness. *Urban Dreams* is a challenge to every urban educator and every urban political and community leader to bring out the remarkable qualities in students under their charge. It is a reminder to parents that it is never too late, that, as one student so eloquently expressed in an essay on respect, seeds planted can thrive once cared for, even if they have been neglected for a while. The stories of hope, resilience, and character that are contained in the essays of *Urban Dreams* give voice to the souls of children and give adults the opportunity to listen, learn, and act.

ABOUT THIS BOOK

Urban Dreams: Stories of Hope, Resilience, and Character is a compilation of essays written by the students of Plainfield to celebrate their sound character, resiliency, and optimism, and to remind us of the impact adults have on children. Indeed, sometimes a very large impact can result from a seemingly small action. We want the readers to understand the process underlying the *Laws of Life*, but, more importantly, to focus on the potential of urban youth and open their minds and hearts to seeing these children in new, deeper, more differentiated and, ultimately, positive ways. Each chapter has a theme based on one *Law of Life* (Love, Responsibility, Respect, Family/ Relationships, Perseverance, Self-Discipline, Courage, Honesty, and Kindness). All nine chapters consist of essays from students in elementary, middle, and/or high school relating to the main theme of the chapter. The essays included here were chosen from among many written over a four-year period of time; some student authors are identified by name, some by pseudonym, others remains anonymous, in keeping with the wishes of their parents/guardians. We have attempted to represent a variety of age levels, genders, and ethnic groups. Many student essays covered more than one *Law of Life*, and hence are not included in this collection. It is important to note that these are not only the essays judged "best," but rather a mix of many. Our aim is to show how, when given the opportunity to do so, most students in urban districts can do very well at reflecting on how they want to live their lives. Each chapter opens with an essay by a member of the community (e.g., the mayor, a school teacher, police officer, school district board member, etc.) who relates his or her own personal story and connects it to the chapter's particular *Law of Life*.

The essays were written in free form; that is, students were ask to think about their *Laws of Life* and encouraged to think about and write their thoughts. Teachers provided input regarding grammar and spelling and reflected back on what students said for clarity; they did not work to modify the content, but rather to improve students' writing. The essays were then shared with peers for "writer's workshop" feedback, brought home to be shared with parents and guardians to stimulate conversations about character, and then completed in school and submitted for ratings. The Superintendent who began the program in Plainfield, Dr. Larry Leverett, sent a letter home to every essay writer, praising them for their work and declaring them a "winner" in the quest for character. Individual schools and the district over-all held *Laws of Life* celebrations to further acknowledge in various ways both the student essayists whose writing was judged to be most exceptional (see the *Appendix for Educators*) and these essays were read aloud at parent-teacher-community gatherings and/or compiled in collections to be distrib-uted to the community. Other elements of the *Laws of Life* approach, in-cluding logos and short slogans put on signs and t-shirts and visual and performing arts events (e.g., artwork, choreography, songwriting) were also encouraged and recognized as a way of broadening children's literacy be-yond the essay writing format.

There was some debate about the title, "*Urban Dreams.*" Some felt that it was wrong to imply that hope and inspiration were uniquely needed by, be-ing provided to, or experienced by urban youth. We were told that the word "urban" might imply "minority" and this could be seen as negative. Others felt that the true common denominator is poverty. Some wanted a more up-lifting title. These and other comments were taken very seriously, and so we point to our subtitle: *Stories of Hope, Resilience, and Character.* The *Laws of Life* are important and accessible to many groups. They are not uniquely ben-eficial to urban youth; we are not implying that urban youth are uniquely in need of hope or that they, alone, have dreams for a better life, or special moral sensitivities.

We believe, however, that our book is a unique attempt to share realistic and uplifting messages grounded in the voice of urban school children. While we do have adults reflecting on their own *Laws of Life*, the focus is clearly the children. They were not specially selected, nor were they individuals with particular resilience, or on some designated track for success. Their future is uncertain. What most people do not realize is how these youth attempt to deal with the difficulties life has thrown at them, the values that they hold, and the importance of nurturing them and their goodness before too many of them succumb to the relentless pressures of negative influences and the sad void of insufficient positive, caring resources. We feel people are ready for a message of hope and inspiration about urban youth.

ABOUT THE EDITORS

Maurice J. Elias, Ph.D. is the senior author of this volume. He is a Professor of Psychology at Rutgers University, a Founding Member of the Leadership

Team of the Collaborative for Academic, Social, and Emotional Learning (www.CASEL.org) and directs the Rutgers Social-Emotional Learning Lab (www.rci.rutgers.edu/~melias/). Gina Ogburn-Thompson is a counselor and Claudine Lewis is a social worker in the Plainfield Public Schools; they have worked with the *Laws of Life* program from its inception over the past five years and have lovingly and carefully nurtured and crafted this program and documented its elements. In this work, they have been aided over the years by many staff members who have served on the *Laws of Life* committee, as well as with student and community essay screeners, judges and donors to various essay recognition events. Deborah I. Neft, Ph.D. served as the Rutgers *Laws of Life* Team Liaison to Plainfield and has been involved in every aspect of implementation, including judging and scoring the essays. Together, we have led the editorial team that has selected the essays for inclusion in Urban Dreams. We also wish to acknowledge the assistance of Cydney Van Dyck, Rebecca Irby, Sara Elias, Linda Cedeno, Andrew Meillers, and Megan Kash in various aspects of the organization, management, and review process as well as the process of securing necessary permissions. Deborah Peterson provided insightful and careful copyediting for this project, for which we are grateful. Lastly, we thank Arthur Schwartz, Peggy Sweeney, Marge Brennan, Kimon Sargeant, and many others at the John Templeton Foundation for their inspiration and continuing encouragement and support.

Chapter One

Kindness

KINDNESS

Judith Cooper-Benjamin

Editors' Note: Judith Benjamin's daughter Monique, whom she discusses below, was the first district-wide winner of the 5th Grade *Laws of Life* essay contest in Plainfield. Her extraordinarily moving essay can be found in Chapter 2 (Courage). Her 8th grade essay, written after much of her middle school experience, can be found in Chapter 3 (Respect). Monique passed away before beginning high school. However, her own kindness, courage, and humanity touched many and continue to do so.

The essence of kindness comes from the heart. The golden rule has always been to treat people the way you want to be treated. There is a gentle spirit that goes along with a person who is kind. Children are taught from the time they are small to be nice to each other. As parents, we are expected to encourage the development of kindness in young people.

Over the past seven years, we have had to deal with my daughter's illness. During that time, we had to handle the good along with the bad. The amount of tears that were shed is immeasurable. But yet there were times when a bright light of kindness was sent our way, a light that made a lot of the difficult times bearable.

As the months turned into years, we lost a lot of our friends and our family became too busy to assist us. We were soon forgotten. It was during those times that we learned that kindness comes in many different degrees. There were many times when we were not treated very nicely; we have had to endure harsh criticism and ridicule. But, still, we had to stand in the face of adversity.

When my daughter entered middle school, her life changed drastically even though she was still battling her illness. The social worker who was assigned to her for that first school year approached her with grace and humility. The kindness that was shown to us was remarkable. After struggling for three years in the school system as well as having problems with the medical team, we did not believe that there was any compassion to be found anywhere.

After several meetings, this young lady approached my daughter's case with a sympathetic but loving nature. She reassured us that things would turn out fine. My daughter started middle school on a positive note. We were able to breathe a sign of relief through the entire school year. My child was able to look forward to each day that she felt well enough to go to school. Not only did Mrs. Grant-Giles make the first year wonderful for Monique, but also she made the entire three years in the Hubbard Middle School a memory that we would never forget.

The kindness that was shown by her teachers was also shown by the students. The fear that had consumed Monique was finally subsiding. A small word or little smile goes a long way in a lonely world. During the last six months, the students and the teachers became our friends. They proved to us that kindness was not just a word, but was a meaningful spirit that was shared among many. When the battle was over and the dust had settled, kindness had blown our way. Kindness became one of our *Laws of Life*.

Life is a gift from God, but kindness is a spirit birthed from the heart.

FORGIVENESS OVERPOWERS HATE

Anonymous, 11th Grade

Most people live their lives based on hate that they have for others. They believe that the only way to survive is to hold up a wall of hate, not letting anyone in but themselves. A lot of people think that their law of life is hate. That is all they have ever learned. Personally, my law of life is "Forgiveness." I think the only way to survive is to forgive. It is the key to happiness.

Many people took the time to learn how to forgive. I took the time to observe how they felt before they forgave someone and how they felt afterwards. My mother showed me that being a bigger person is being able to forgive. Throughout my mother's life she never practiced hatred. She showed love for anyone she thought needed it. She always told me "If you see someone who feels nothing but hate, pray for them. And hope that one day some kind of happiness comes into their lives." She thought that to hate someone is only to hate yourself. So I'm trying to change my ways, so I can be at a better place, and be able to put myself in better surroundings.

All my life I practiced nothing but hate. I had hate for everyone that I thought hated me, and for anyone who hated themselves. I had to learn the hard way that hate brings nothing but misery. I stayed to myself until I couldn't take it anymore. I decided to forgive anyone who had done any wrong doing to me, hoping to find myself in the process. Later on in life, I forgave every wrong thing that anyone had done to me. In return, I asked God to give me happiness. And to my surprise he did just that!

In order to forgive, you have to learn how to understand what other people are going though. The easiest thing to do is to hate someone or something. The hardest thing to do is learning to forgive someone. To me, forgiveness is not just saying "I forgive you." It means understanding what the person did and why they did it. And how can you take their weakness and try to help them make themselves stronger?

I realized that hate only disowns someone for their own faults. Everyone is human. How could I honestly disown someone for their weakness, when I myself have my own faults? To blame someone for a mistake is not human and, in my eyes, everyone is the same. You can never think that you are better than anyone else. Forgiveness is will power and love. It is a communication with someone on a higher level even though they show weakness. Forgiveness is helping someone in their time of need.

I chose to forgive rather than the hate. I no longer look down upon anyone. Being able to help people take their hate and help them become a stronger person is what makes me happy. It makes them a stronger person, and in the process makes me a stronger person also. Being able to forgive is the greatest gift in the world. So, you understand why "Forgiveness" is my Law of Life. Remember it's easier to forgive, than to learn how to hate.

APPRECIATION: THROUGH HER EYES

Anonymous, 8th Grade

Tanya sat and watched as her Grandma Cicely a knitted her a brand new winter sweater. She sat in her favorite rocking chair by the window. Tanya enjoyed those times with her grandmother. Her mother would take her to her grandmother's house to spend a day or two. Grandma Cicely would bake cookies and do what grandmothers usually do. She would make cherry flavored Kool-Aid and fried chicken. The house always smelled of food, love and hospitality. Tanya loved it.

Only July 21, 2004, Cicely Janelle Eleanor Wilson passed away, losing her long battle with breast cancer. Tanya was crushed. After Grandma Cicely's death, Tanya's mom thought it would be best if they moved into her house instead of selling it. As Tanya watched the movers move her things into her grandma's house, the pain inside her grew more and more unbearable. Tanya sat in the kitchen crying. She thought of the time Grandma Cicely told her stories of when she had sat in her spot in the kitchen. Her grandmother would tell her about times of when she was growing, up during segregation in the South. She told her about sitting and watching Martin Luther King, Jr. deliver his "I Have a Dream" speech.

Tanya's tears flowed just as her grandmother's love flowed in her heart. Tanya's mom, Ada Wilson, sat in the old rocking chair by the window in the living room thinking of her mother. Ada called to her daughter to help her rearrange the living room. As Tanya walked in, she felt a dark feeling come over her. "Mom, what is that chair still doing here?!" Tanya exclaimed.

"Tanya, this was your grandmother's favorite chair. I'm not getting rid of this rocking chair." her mother argued.

"Ma, that thing is repulsive. It's…"

"Don't you speak that way of this chair!" Her mother began to become angry at this point. "You know your grandmother loved this chair. Don't you dare say that again!" Her mother stormed off into the den. Tanya sat down in the chair. She began to smile as the memories of her grandmother in that chair began to flow back into her mind. Tanya sat and thought about the *Laws of Life* essay she had to write. She found her inspiration in this incident. She began to write her essay on her grandma's old flowered notepad. It came out this way:

Appreciation is often an action that we miss. Sometimes it takes a great loss, sometimes just a small act for something to be appreciated. For me, appreciation came easy until the passing of my loving grandmother, the honorable Cicely Janelle Eleanor Wilson, better known as Grandma Cicely. That loss in my life opened my eyes to certain things. My grandmother was a soldier in her own time. She has had her trials and tribulations but I know life was worth it for her.

She bore 5 children and had 13 grandchildren and 5 great-grandchildren. She was so pleased to find out about all of us. I know that she has given up a lot to make sure that her children and their children had what they needed. Sometimes we worked her last nerve and she beat us to the high heavens, but we know she did it out of love. She always did everything out of love.

When she died a few months ago, I knew my life wouldn't be the same without her. She was the rock of the Wilson family. She always made sure we were right and there was no tension between any of us. She did anything for us. If we wanted or needed anything, she would be the one to get it or give it to us. She never said no to anyone. She was the neighborhood mom.

Lately, I've been a bit edgy and it showed today. My mom was sitting Grandma Cicely's rocking chair. Oh, how she loved that chair! When I saw my mother sitting in the chair, a sudden dark feeling came over me. I snapped at her. I knew it was wrong, but I couldn't control myself. I sat down in the chair and thought about what my grandmother would say to me if she saw me do that. I knew she wouldn't approve. She would beat my butt all up and down that living room. That was when I found my law of life.

I learned I should appreciate not the finer things in life, but the things with inner value and things you would usually overlook. Sometimes we do this because we have no appreciation for those things. When we learn to appreciate them, they earn value in our eyes and become more a part of our life. How can something with no money-value be the most valuable treasure in your life? That's easy. We learn to appreciate such things. After that incident, I knew that my grandmother would be there to reach me through her spirit. She would be my guide as she had for my fourteen years of life already. She would keep me going the right way, help me to learn how to be appreciative of what I have, what I've learned and what is in store for me in the future. I will realize that those things will become valuable because they were appreciated.

KINDNESS IS DOING FOR OTHERS

Alexandria Livingston, 5th Grade

A wise man once said, 'Be the change you want to see in the world.' This means that you have to care about and be considerate of others; then others might catch on. My parents have impressed this upon me. They have taught me to be responsible and to have integrity. This quote and these values helped my sister and me face a situation that demonstrated what my parents shared with me.

"Call 1-800-Feed-A-Child. Not helping the children today…no progress tomorrow." That's how it all started. Our empathy for children less fortunate surfaced. After watching that commercial, my sister told me that she wants to help kids like those shown on TV. Their ribs showed that they were starving. Their faces were long and their eyes had a hint of sadness behind them. My sister and I went upstairs to write a note for my mother. We didn't want to forget the number or lose our train of thought, so we wrote a note instead of telling. It read:

Dear Mom,

Please call this number, 1-800-Feed-A-Child. The commercial was so sad, and if we send money then children can eat better and they won't be so skinny. We really want to help these children. This would mean a lot to us.

Yours truly,

I took the note to my mother and waited for an answer. She dialed the number and asked for all the information. I went upstairs to tell my sister the good news. When I told her, her eyes lit up and we both yelled, "YES!" Before I knew it, both my dresser and hers were almost empty. We went through the drawers and took out all the clothes that were too small. Our usually full shoe rack was almost empty because we took all the shoes that were too small and put them in a big box along with the clothes. We also packed up the toys that we didn't play with any longer. Any loose change we found around the house we put in an old eyeglass case. Before we knew it we had $15.15 to send the hungry children. We were on our way to helping the children who didn't have much to eat or wear. My sister looked at me and told me that she cares for them, and wants them to have as many things as they need, as many as we can give them. I could tell she was about to cry. Through this experience we better understood the quote, "Be the change you want to see in the world."

"Life's most persistent and urgent question: What are you doing for others?" This is a quote by Martin Luther King, Jr. My sister and I have tried to rise to this challenge. We understand that we have to try to make a difference in someone's life if we want to make our world a better place to live in. Everyone should live peacefully, whether it be finding a home or overcoming other obstacles in his or her life. This is my Law of Life. Everyone should have one that means a lot to him or her.

CARE FOR THE WORLD

Kianja Jackson, 5th Grade

What would the world be like if there were no old people? *There would be no world.*

You may think that old people are just bums on the street if they are not of your relatives. I mean, you love your grandparents and great-grandparents, right? But if people are not family or friends, you could care less about them. Sometimes I feel this way, but often, in fact most of the time, I feel very sympathetic for them.

This feeling of sympathy comes and goes in my mind. It is very hurtful to me. It is hurtful because I can't stand the fact that the government can take old people's houses away from them. They know that the particular person may not be able to pay to keep the house, because they either have no job or they don't make enough money to keep their house. Also, it's not like they can work two jobs. They get very tired and ARE in bad condition. They are not able to really work EVEN one job. Do they have to go to nursing and retirement homes? In such places, residents don't get the care they want and need.

Some of you reading my paper may call me crazy or idiotic for writing about old people. But that's just it. We don't care about our senior citizens. Do you want the world to care about you when you grow old? I used some of my friends' opinions to prove my point. None of them said they would not want the young people to care about them. I think you would say the same thing.

Do you know how hard it is to be old? You think you do, but you really don't. In our everyday lives an old person dies. When you become older and older, you also become more and more handicapped, not only physically but socially and emotionally.

I mean there are bills that seniors can't pay. Their mortgage may increase by a few hundred dollars and if they can't pay, they become homeless. What can they do? They don't have a job.

To see old people on the street and not able to get their supplies, just makes me want to cry inside. These feelings I cannot hide.

TREAT PEOPLE THE WAY YOU WANT TO BE TREATED

Eric Shaw, 5th Grade

My teacher makes us read a lot of books and watch a lot of videos about Black History. That's how I found out about the ideals that Dr. Martin Luther King really stood for. Discovering Dr. King has forced me to think about my life and how I was living. When I read his "I have a dream" speech I began to think about his words, especially the part where he talks about treating people the way you want to be treated.

There is a boy in my class whom I have not always treated with dignity and respect. I called him names and once I blamed him for something he didn't do. I accused him of taking my computer disk without my permission and losing it. I screamed at him and said bad things to him that didn't make him feel so good. I know how it feels when people say bad things to you because I've had it done to me. After a conversation with my teacher, I began to think about how others must feel when I mistreat them. She asked me think about Dr. King's speech and whether I was living the kind of life he would be proud of and whether I was proud of myself. I wasn't proud of what I had one. I'm trying to change my ways and treat people the same we way I want to be treated. I know how it feels to be mistreated and I'm not happy about the way I've made others feel.

Reading Dr. King's speech has changed my life and I now believe that it is important to treat people with respect. Dr. King said, "We must not allow our creative protest to degenerate into physical violence." I'm working on self-control and trying hard not to get a bad attitude with people when someone says something I don't like.

Dr. Martin Luther King has a special day called Dr. King day. It is not just any day, but one on which we celebrate the life and legacy of a man who brought hope and healing to America. He did that by never giving up and never giving in to violence. From this day forward, I will celebrate Dr. King's life by obeying my parents and staying out of trouble and treating people the way I want to be treated. Like Dr. King, I've decided to become an agent of change. This is my law of life.

HELP THOSE IN NEED

Stella Oleforo, 5th Grade

I chose kindness as my law of life. When I was ten, I would always help this lady by getting her groceries. She could barely walk and talk. When I first met her, she told me that she would like it if I helped her with her groceries. She told me that if I did, she would pay me, but I said, "No." I know that I would not help her for money. I would do this out of kindness. I began going to the store for her if she needed and continued to help her with her groceries.

Whenever I left after helping her, I would begin to think of the things that could have happened to her if I was not here. Helping people is a good deed. I knew that this was a good thing to do and besides it was fun. I had taught myself to be kind. A few days after, I heard that she died. Later, I was told that her house had been sold. My memories of her are that she was a real nice lady and she didn't ask for much. She never left her house much either, but she was still just like everyone else. The one thing that I will always have in my heart and my soul is that one lady. I *really* liked her. I know that kindness and good deeds pay off. I bet she is smiling down at me from heaven and saying, "Everything will be okay!"

The lesson I learned from this is that being kind is important, especially when you can help people in need. This is my law of life essay. Starting today, make sure to include kindness in your world.

Chapter Two

Courage

COURAGE

Herbert T. Green is a Resident Reader in the Plainfield, NJ, public schools.

Courage is defined in the Encarta College Dictionary as "the ability to face danger, difficulty, uncertainty, or pain without being overcome by fear or being deflected from a chosen course of action." Baldomero Lopez comes to my mind instantly as an example of courage. He was a classmate of mine at the United States Naval Academy more than sixty years ago, and died in action on September 15, 1950 in the Korean War. Baldomero was awarded the Congressional Medal of Honor for his "exceptional courage, fortitude and devotion to duty [which] reflected the highest credit upon 1st Lt. Lopez and the U.S. Naval Service. He gallantly gave his life for his country." The Congressional Medal of Honor is the highest honor awarded to an individual serving in the Armed Services for valor in action against an enemy. I can still remember grieving for the loss of a friend and at the same time bursting with pride at the fact that he "faced danger" without being overcome by fear. His selfless action saved the lives of many Marines under his command.

I also think of the heroes and heroines who worked so hard in the name of civil rights. African-Americans of all ages and their White allies earned our admiration for fearlessly confronting racist resistance to court-ordered integration. I can still see Elizabeth Eckford, one of the nine Black students seeking court-ordered admittance to Central High School in Little Rock, Arkansas in September 1957, being confronted by National Guardsmen with drawn bayonets and crowds shouting, "Lynch her." This beautiful, dignified, and courageous fifteen-year-old girl and her friends brought racist Governor

Faubus to his knees and awakened President Eisenhower to the need for action by the federal government. It was the time of Mrs. Rosa Parks' refusal to give up her seat on the bus to a White man, as well as of the emergence of the 27-year old Dr. Martin Luther King, Jr. as our greatest civil rights leader. It was also an era in which courageous college students staged non-violent "sit-ins" at food counters and were not "deflected from their chosen course of action" by racist thugs. In 1963, the civil rights leaders took on Birmingham, Alabama, the most segregated city in America. The city had had 60 unsolved racial bombings since the end of World War II, but it, too, could not withstand the determination and bravery of the courageous civil rights leaders.

There are endless examples of the courageous behavior of good people who have changed the lives of many others, but my point here is clear. Over the course of a blessedly long lifetime, I have observed with growing admiration the actions of these individuals and have concluded from this that courage has become an important Law of my Life. So, I try to speak out against injustice wherever I see it and support the efforts of those who are organized to work for change, especially for changes which can help those who are disadvantaged. In my everyday life, I work to improve the educational opportunities for poor and minority children. This advocacy has often brought me into conflict with important governmental and community figures, but I have always stood my ground, in large part because I have become aware that courage has become a Law of my Life.

To conclude, one observation that I send especially to young readers of this book and of my essay: It would be wrong to assume that courage can only be demonstrated by overt actions such as those described above. In our everyday contacts with others, we demonstrate this virtue more often than we realize. Sometimes we show it not by what we do, but by what we refuse to do. Never miss the opportunity to speak out against injustice or dishonesty or cruelty, and do your best to not participate in such actions when you see them happening around you.

COURAGE HELPS YOU ENDURE LIFE'S DIFFICULTIES

Ashley Johnson, 11th Grade

One look at my niece and you could tell she was sick. Her usual energetic nine-year old body was a lifeless pile of bones. We rushed her to Muhlenberg Hospital after her temperature reached over 100 degrees. We sat waiting in the lobby until the doctor told us the heart-wrenching news: Briana had diabetes. As I sat on her bed in the pediatric ward, I broke down. I wondered how she would endure life.

Diabetes is a disease in which the body does not produce or properly use insulin. Insulin is a hormone that is needed to convert sugar, starches and other food into energy needed for daily life. When my niece contracted this disease, her life changed dramatically. No more sugar. No more this or that. All of the little things that a normal kid could enjoy were now off limits. Sugar and sweets were a major part of her (or any nine year old's) life and suddenly this was all taken away from her. When I realized this, I was very sad and upset. I thought of how she would feel every time she witnessed someone eating sugar. As a 13 year old, it would be hard for me to resist it, so how would she be able to?

One day while I was at the hospital, I watched as my niece pricked her fingertips, and then injected herself with two needles. I excused myself to go to the rest room, and when I returned, she was lying on her bed in tears. "I wish I was born over again" she cried. This left me heartbroken. A nine- year old child is supposed to enjoy life, not despise it.

That day, we made a pledge. Since she could no longer eat sweets, I promised her that I would eat fewer sweets. Seeing how brave she was providing me with a law of life that I truly cherish: Courage. I define courage as staying strong even in the toughest times. Even when you feel like dropping your head and giving up, you keep on trying.

When I saw how brave she was in dealing with her sickness, I was inspired to be brave and courageous, too. This is a lesson I remind myself of constantly. Whether I'm in school, out of school, or at home, I try to show courage and incorporate it into my daily routine.

For example, I pledged to lower my sugar intake and I have tried to. At home, I have cut down on eating sugars and sweets. I also drink diet soda. This is really hard because I have a store across the street so I am tempted to buy candy. But I try to have courage and stay strong. When I am with my friends, I also try to practice this. I am not perfect, but I am certainly trying.

There are many times when it would be easier for me to give up. I am not perfect. I play basketball and sometimes I mess up and don't do the right thing. My easiest option would be to give up when I make mistakes, but I don't. When I think of how brave my niece is, it puts it all in perspective. I CAN'T give up. I HAVE to be brave. I CAN'T let her down. What would it say about me as a person, an aunt, or a friend if I disappointed her like that? I couldn't do that.

I am being taught by a nine-year old. Even though I am 13 and a straight-A student, a 3rd grader is teaching me life lessons. Her bravery is an inspiration for me.

She has had to learn to regulate her body sugar because if she doesn't, there will be terrible consequences. She has to accept the fact that what may be good now, such as candy, will harm her in the long run. As for me, I need to have the courage to make good decisions. Even though these decisions will be hard for me now, in due course, they will turn out positively.

THE COURAGE I HAVE

Justin Reyes, 5th Grade

The most important thing in life to me is courage. It means being brave or meeting danger without fear. The first time I found courage, I was in third grade at the YMCA. It was a foggy and dreary afternoon. I was playing tag happily with my friends. I was running as fast as a rabbit and then, BAM! I hit my head on a shiny pointy needle. I was crying like my brother when he doesn't want to go to school. The staff cleaned my head and they called my parents to come.

When I looked up, I saw a puddle of blood. My dad came and rushed me to the hospital as fast as a cheetah. When we got there I found out I had to get stitches. My eyes and mouth were wide. It took a long time waiting in the waiting room. I started to get very worried. I thought to myself, "I have to be brave. I have to be brave." When I was in the operating groom, I laid down comfortably staring at the shiny light above me.

My dad said, "Be brave. It will be done in a little while."

I continued thinking to myself, "I have to be brave. I have to be brave." Soon it was all done. It didn't hurt a lot. Then I felt happy. That is how I found my courage.

Another challenge in my life, a time when I needed courage, was when I was in a big race at school. I was looking forward to this race for a while. I always wanted to be the fastest person in my school. It was a sunny summer day. When we arrived at the field I found out that I was picked to be in a short race before the big one. I lost. I came in last place. While I was running, I felt like I was being sucked through a black hole. I thought, "I'll never win the big race now."

I was feeling down the entire day. Finally, the time for the big race arrived. I was frightened. I was nervous that I would lose and feel silly in front of all my classmates. I walked out on the track and got in my lane. Then, "Ready, Set, Go!" I was running like a cheetah dashing here and there. I was in last place. Then I said to myself, "You can do it. Believe in yourself." I began to run faster. I passed the other runners. Finally I crossed the finish line. I came in second place!!!!! I was as happy as a dog with a bone. That's when I found out that I could use courage anytime and any-where.

Having courage in my heart helps me to get through tough times. Courage is a key to life. I can use courage when doing school work, when playing sports, when being punished and when running a race. If you want courage, you need faith in yourself.

COURAGE IS OVERCOMING YOUR FEARS

Dayner Davis, 5th Grade

Courage is a very important law that simply means you are brave. Brave enough to do what you need to do. My own experience was when I had to transfer to a new school. This happened last year in 4th grade during the month of February. My mother took me to the office of Emerson Elementary and I got signed up for a class I had never been to before.

I was a little nervous at first because I did not know anyone, but I found the courage to go in that room and take care of my business. The teacher gave me an assignment which took her class a week to do. But it only took me a day. She gave me very nice compliments. At the time, most of the kids were being very mean to me. I guess they were jealous of my intelligence but I did not let it get to me because I had enough courage to be myself.

My role model was my mom. She told me not to worry and to do what I had to do. Not only this, but I have also seen her being courageous herself. Even though she has a lot of troubles and difficulties in her life, she manages to overcome those dilemmas she has.

Courage is important because if you have it then nothing will keep you from doing what you have to do. Nothing will prevent you from overcoming your fears or problems and no one will ever call, or even think of calling, you a coward or a chicken.

Courage is something that is in everyone. Even if you do not show it, you still have it. For example, you have the courage to pass a test. Or, if someone pressures you to do something you know is not right, you have the courage to say "no." And, you really have the courage to do anything you want to do, nothing can stop you.

I am not going to lie: Sometimes I am not brave. Other times I prove to everyone and to myself that I can be very courageous.

Courage is a very important law of life. It will always be important in my life, no matter what.

BEING BRAVE IS NOT EASY, BUT IT'S NECESSARY

Monique Cooper-Benjamin, 5th Grade

To have courage means to be able to face life with confidence and bravery. When I first became sick I was scared. My face changed. It became very fat with a lot of hair on it. All the pills I was taking caused this. I didn't want to go back to school because I knew that the kids would laugh at me. I didn't want to face the fact that I was sick. My mom told me to have faith in myself, and believe that as long as I treat others right the same would happen for me. So I went back to school and the kids did point at me. Some even acted like they were scared of me. But I stood up to the challenge. Sometimes you have to have the courage to do things even when you are afraid. School became a lonely place for me because the kids didn't want to be with me. But I have learned that courage is a major part of life. You have to hold your head up and go foreword. Life brings many struggles, but you must be determined to do what is right. Because the kids have not treated me right doesn't mean that I can't treat them right. I must treat them the way I want to be treated. My mom says that I am a very brave girl. But the truth is sometimes I don't want to be brave. To have the courage to walk in the room where everyone is looking at you is hard. It is harder when people are talking about you even when you can them. But God has given me the courage and strength to hold on. To have courage means you have to be in control of your actions. For example, being able to step forward when things are bad. I am eleven years old and I have to face a lot of pain and tough times. I am now doing dialysis three times a week and I feel sick all the time. I would not wish this on anyone. I have to accept responsibility for dealing with my illness. Being sick does not excuse me from my school work or chores. In the three years that I've been sick, I have learned a lot about myself and others. My actions are what counts. Being able to step to the plate and be accountable is hard but necessary. There are a lot of things that I can no longer do like riding a bike. Writing a lot is hard, too, but I still must face life head on. When I fall sometimes I don't want to get back up. But then I think about the kids who have cancer. Their life is harder than mine. So, I struggle to go on. To have the courage to stand takes a lot of faith in God. We all need to stop and think: Are we willing to have courage in the time of trouble? Being brave is not easy, but it's necessary.

STAY STRONG

Tonju Hunt, 5th Grade

Have you ever had to go through seeing your mom go in and out of the hospital? My "Law of Life" talks about how I struggled to stay strong and not break down in front of my family. It was a few years ago when I was living on Franklin Place, a street located in Plainfield, New Jersey. My mom was out of remission, and I was really too young to know what that meant. She wasn't feeling all that good that year, and she was crawling back and forth to the bathroom. She then told me that she had Crohn's Disease. Crohn's Disease causes inflammation in the lower intestine, called the ileum. However, it can affect any part of the digestive tract from the mouth to the anus. Crohn's disease is an inflammatory bowel disease (I.B.D.).

My sister and I cared for my mother in her time of need. We gave her pills, sandwiches, and water. At that time, I didn't know what was going to happen to her. I was only four years of age, and I didn't understand why this was happening to my mom.

When we moved back to my grandma's house, my mom got worse, and she kept going back and forth to the doctor. Living at my grandmother's house was a little easier on my sister and I, since she was able to help us out with my mother. As I got older, I started to understand my mom's disease.

Her condition was up and down, like a seesaw. In the year 1998, she needed surgery. The surgery would alleviate her pain. It was a scary year for all of us, because the doctor said that she had only one month to live, if she refused the surgery. "Die!" I screamed silently in my head. I couldn't believe what I was hearing. The thought of my mother not being here with me was heart wrenching. I started to cry. I felt pain and fear in my heart. My mom told me not to worry, and that everything would work out.

Even though I am the youngest child, my older sister didn't really understand my mom's condition and how serious it was. She also didn't understand how sad I really felt deep down inside. My mom told me to stay strong. She said that if she were to die, my sister and I had each other, and that she would always be with us in spirit. The day of the surgery, I was a nervous wreck. I was jumpy, and couldn't think straight. I felt as if I was going to have a nervous break down. Every time I was about to cry, a vision of my mom would appear and whisper, "Stay strong." I told myself to stay strong because I know she wouldn't have wanted it any other way.

As time slowly passed, we waited patiently in the hospital for the doctors to return with information regarding my mother. The waiting room was so quiet that you could have heard a pin drop. The doctor later came in, and we were excited and worried at the same time. We were so excited that we didn't let the doctor say anything. Then, silence came over the room. The doctor said that she survived the surgery, and that she would be in a whole lot of pain for a few days, and that we had to take real good care of her. I was so relieved. It was like the happiest day of my life. Even though she wasn't going to come home right away, I was still happy to know that she was going to live, and that God gave her another chance. The first year of remission, my mom did not feel pain in her stomach at all. The second and third years were not very good for her because the Crohn's Disease came back.

She got treatments on a regular basis to help keep the disease tamed. I was very disappointed to hear that she was not well again. I wish that she could have stayed in remission. This summer my mom went to the hospital and I knew the drill. But this time she went in an ambulance, and that was one of the worst things happening at that time. Each time she went to the hospital, I was there with her. During that time, I really didn't want to be bothered by anybody. I went to the hospital everyday until she came home. I had fun doing that and seeing my mom recover from her sickness.

In spite of all the pain that my mom endures, she continues to show me that she has kept the strength that was passed on to me, her descendant. She can spend time with us as a mother, friend, and companion. My mom is the "Love of my Life." I have always survived with a smile. I love you Mommy.

STRENGTH IN DIFFICULT TIMES

Jillian Herrera Bonilla, 5th Grade

My Law of Life is strength. I learned how to be strong when my mother needed surgery. Being strong was difficult because sometimes I felt sad. Strength is what I needed when my mom faced her surgery alone.

Mom made an appointment with the doctor because something was wrong with her eye. When we went to the doctor's office, the doctor checked it. When the doctor told her what was wrong she gave me a worried look. The doctor asked her if she wanted surgery or a dead eye. I was hoping that she would choose the surgery.

She went to another office to find out about the surgery. "How about June 11th?" The doctor asked. My mom looked at me. She knew what was going to happen on that day. The doctor was trying to figure out what day June 11th fell on. I informed him that it was on a Wednesday. The doctor was surprised. My mom told the doctor that it was my birthday.

Two months passed, and it was time for mom's surgery. I was worried, nervous, and scared, so were my friend and her mom. I didn't know what to do until my mom got out of surgery. When they called her name, I looked deeply into her eyes. You could see that she was scared. She said that everything was going to be alright and that she was going to be fine.

My mom was in the operating room for more than 2 hours. I was wondering what they were doing to her. When they said the surgery was done, they let my friend, her mom, and me inside to see her. The eye she had surgery on was covered with a patch. My mom looked tired. They offered her something to eat or drink, she said she only wanted something to drink. They gave her pills for the pain. I was happy that she was okay and able to go home. Now my mom doesn't have the red thing in her eye, and she can see better than before. She has to use eye drops everyday.

My mom's surgery is something that I will remember for the rest of my life, because it taught me how to be strong. I learned that I needed to have strength for something hurtful that was going on in my life. Even though my mom was fearful, she didn't show it. I learned how to be strong from watching her when she was going through a scary time in her life. I stood by my mom's side because I wanted to show her that I could be as strong for her. Although I wanted to cry at the time, I knew I couldn't. My mom has taught me this, and I would like to show other people they can do it, too.

Chapter Three

Respect

THE MEANING OF RESPECT

Dr. Jose Adames, Provost and Assistant Vice-President, Plainfield Campus, Union County College

Before joining Union County College, I worked for sixteen years as a faculty member and as an administrator at a local university. My last position was that of Dean of Liberal Arts. As dean, I handled many kinds of unexpected situations including faculty-student issues. I am a morning person and therefore I was accustomed to getting early to the office before anyone else. The early morning is a good time to organize the day's work, to do reading or writing, and to reflect. Early one morning before any of the staff had arrived, a faculty member burst into my office with a student. His face was flush red and he looked visibly agitated. Before I could finish the phrase, "Good morning. . . what seems to be the problem?" he turned to a young woman who had followed him into my office. He insisted that I remove her from his history course because the student arrived late for the second time in the semester! He then walked out of the office. The young woman was visibly upset.

At that moment, I had several choices. I could have insisted that the faculty member return to my office; I could have left the problem to the department chair to resolve; or, I could have taken the student's contact information and had the assistant to the dean handle the issue when he arrived. I chose none of these. I wanted this student to know that at that very moment someone at the university cared enough to listen. I set aside the papers I had been working on and asked her to sit down. I introduced myself and asked her to tell me her name and explain what had occurred this morning.

I listened for twenty minutes without interruption as she apologized and explained why she had been late to the class. She talked about her mother and the heart attacked that forced her into intensive care at a local hospital three weeks ago. She also told me of the father who had passed away in an automobile accident a few years earlier and of the brother that she now had to take care of, drop off at kindergarten before coming to class, and later pick up on those days when her grandfather could not. In addition, she told me of the full time load of courses she was carrying and her fear of losing her scholarship. Although all of this was clearly causing her great stress, she had kept it all to herself because she did not want anyone else to know about her family's situation or to feel pity for her.

I would never have known the depth of the problems she was facing had I not authenticated her presence as a human being by listening. Far too often, in our rush to meet deadlines or to get to that next meeting, we miss opportunities to affirm the humanity of others by pausing to listen and understand.

Far too often when we make decisions, we think only about OUR own needs and feelings and not about how our decisions impact on others. Respecting someone's feelings consists of asking them how they feel, validating their feelings, empathizing with them, seeking to better understand them, and taking their feelings into consideration in any decision that one makes. This stands in stark contrast to how Ralph Ellison's nameless narrator was treated in *Invisible Man*.

Respect also means accepting the other person for who they are and to take them seriously and give them worth and value. In other words, this means "acknowledging" or "validating" the other person, accepting their individuality. Respect is something that is earned by doing some of the things I just described. It cannot be demanded or forced, though unfortunately some believe that this is the way to receive it. In my view, in order to appreciate and respect others, each person must be aware of their own feelings and be able to express them, and also understand why they feel as they do. They must know how to validate the feelings of others and earnestly believe that feelings are important and have value. Most importantly, they must be able to actively listen to the opinions of others and try to find common ground without making hasty judgments.

As a judge in the *Laws of Life* program, I have learned a great deal by reading about the heartfelt experiences and beliefs of our young people and, also from listening to the "voices" each of the writers, the feelings and convictions expressed by their stories or by a particular term used. Equally as important is that which is left unsaid. An essay I read recently talked about the importance of citizenship and respect. The student wrote about the laws she would teach her children when she becomes a parent, laws that she hadn't "used enough" when she was their age. One of those laws concerned the importance of respecting one's parents: "My dad taught me that I should never be disrespectful to him or my mother because it would take years off of my life. I believe that this is true, and I will teach this to my children." She was indeed right when she wrote, "it is easier to tell somebody how to do something than it is for you to do it. I hope that my children will understand that respect and citizenship are very important."

Another student wrote about respect and willingness to listen. "Always be willing to listen to others and be willing to allow people to listen to you."

Finally, one student essay addressed the rights of children: "…I believe that we children should be respected in all countries of the world and that adults should be responsible with our lives." She further wrote, "I believe that there is a lack of respect for children and their rights, and that in many instances they are exploited by their own parents" - an amazing statement from a 5th grader!

These essays have caused me to reflect on my own life, experiences and values. They have reminded me of the importance of always validating the person with whom I am interacting, and have reaffirmed that, as the title of Nkosi Johnson's recently published book states, *We are All the Same.*

IF YOU GIVE IT, YOU'LL GET IT

Monique Cooper-Benjamin, 8th Grade

The greatest Law of Life is having "RESPECT." To get respect, you must be able to give it. Life comes with a lot of burdens, but if you have respect for yourself then you can look in the mirror every morning and face the day with grace.

When I go to school and watch the kids mistreat the teacher and the other students, I wonder if they were taught to respect their elders or, more importantly, themselves. Being a kid is hard, but becoming an adult is going to be harder, so we must first learn to respect ourselves then we can gracefully respect each other.

I had to learn the hard way that respect comes in many different forms. Sometimes when I get up in the morning my body hurts and I have to force myself to go to school. I would take my feelings out on people and that was not right. One day a boy in my class was whispering and pointing at me. The teacher noticed and told him that it was very disrespectful to talk about another person either to their face or behind their back. I realized then that my behavior was just as rude as his.

I can hold my head high in the times of trouble since I respect not only my-self, but you too!

CHANGING MY ATTITUDE

Anonymous, 8th Grade

Respect means that I can talk to someone about anything and they won't laugh or make fun of me. I have respect for my classroom assistant. She has taught me to add, subtract, shown me the families of facts and also taught me to round numbers and use the first digits. If it weren't for her, I wouldn't know anything. Now she and I are working on my attitude.

I have a bad attitude. My family says that when I was born, I was dropped on my head. My family laughs at me and asks me, "If I am going to grow up." But my assistant respects me and told me I should respect my family. I can tell her anything and she can tell me things. I love her with all my heart. She does things for me and I appreciate what she does for me. She's my heart.

Sometimes I sit back and think of what has happened to me and sometimes I cry. I am going to stay in school. I am going to finish school and then I am going to college. I am going to go to nursing school and try to get a job at Robert Wood Johnson Hospital.

Because I am in special education, I used to be ashamed to go to the school assembly. I thought that they would laugh at me. Sometimes I cried and they would look at me and think that I was crazy. Now that I am growing up, I am not ashamed to go to the assembly. I remember what my assistant always says: "Don't worry about them. They don't know you and they don't live with you. You know the truth about yourself."

I have been working hard to get out of special education. I have been work-ing hard on my math by getting A's and B's. Also, I am getting A+'s on my spelling tests. This is helping me with my attitude and it helps me to respect myself. I may not be perfect yet, but my assistant is working with me. I am learning to respect myself and other people. Before I started changing my at-titude I wanted to fight people. Now I respect people and, instead of fighting, I walk away.

Even though I am in special education, I am learning a lot more than in the other classes. So I don't care if they make fun of me. Now I respect myself. I have learned a lot about respect from my assistant. I know to leave every-body alone. I know I will get along better with my family and friends because I learned respect.

RESPECT COMES FROM THE HEART

Anonymous, 8th Grade

Respect is something that my dad has always taught me to have. He says that I should respect who and what I am. He says that I should have respect for him and my mom because they have always loved and supported me. He taught me to have respect for my elders who share their knowledge and wisdom with me. Respect is my law of life.

Respect comes from the heart. Every person's heart is like a tree. When a baby is born, his heart is a seed in soil. At this point, all it needs is a main character trait (kindness, generosity, etc.) for its roots and trunk. Some of the *Laws of Life* that the baby needs to believe in will become the branches. In order for the tree to grow, it will need the care of parents, water, and sunlight. If you use pure water and bright sunlight to grow that seed, it will have the roots of respect and a caring attitude toward the world, and it will help this planet to become a better place. If the seed is raised in bitter water and dim sunlight, then it will grow dark and rotten, and it won't do anything but take up space.

Respect is not just treating someone right in order to get something in return. It asks that we treat people the way we want to be treated, fairly and equally. No one wants to be treated like dirt. We all want to be treated with dignity. Respect is showing someone kindness and not trying to hurt them in any way. That is what respect is.

But to gain respect, you have to give it first. In order to give respect, you must respect yourself. People who don't respect themselves often go bad, and they don't care about what becomes of anyone or anything, not even themselves. People like that often find themselves in gangs or they end up as thieves or drug dealers. They don't care what happens to anyone or anything, and they definitely have no respect for others. People who care about themselves and have self-respect find it easy to respect others. They can care about the baby they're looking after or the dog they are walking without worrying about their paycheck. These people have a future.

We live in a really messed up world. So many people lack respect for others. If people had more respect for everything and everyone in the world, there would be no war. There would be no killings, no thieves, no gangs, no need for police and the Twin Towers would still be standing. It's actually kind of sad. The world has gone through many slave trades, wars, revolts, battles, racism, and much more. Many have lost their lives for liberty and the good life.

Respect is my law of life, and it is a very important one for the world. The level of respect that each of us shows can help determine the quality of our life in the world. Since there are so many dark trees with no branches of respect, the world is messed up and full of hate and selfishness. But this is not everywhere, and luckily, there is not enough of it to spread across the entire world. If everyone had respect for their past, their peers, and their lives, the world would be a better place.

SHOW RESPECT – IT WILL FEEL GOOD

Anonymous, 5th Grade

My parents teach me many things. They always say, "Treat others the way you want to be treated. You are a model of us, so you must be respectful." Respect is one thing I want to remember and to show in my everyday life.

A respectful person believes it's always important to listen to and have an open mind when dealing with others. As children, we are taught to respect our parents, teachers, and elders, and to obey school rules, traffic laws, family cultural traditions, be aware of other people's feelings, rights, honor our country's flag, leaders, the truth, and people with different opinions. To me, respect is like a boomerang; you must give it out before it will come back.

One way you can show respect for others is by not leaving the room when someone is speaking. I wish this respect was shown more often in church. Every Sunday when I am in church you can expect two or three people to get up out of their seats and leave the room while the pastor is preaching. It makes me angry everytime this happens because they are not showing respect. To show respect in the church, everyone should remain quietly in their seat until he is finished.

Another way you can show respect for others is by taking a person's feelings into consideration. I remember one day when I was sitting in a fast food restaurant in New York and a homeless man walked in. Right away the waitress started screaming loudly and told the man he had to leave. She did not care whether he had money or not. Everyone in the restaurant looked up to see what was happening. I believe the man felt embarrassed and ashamed. Suddenly, he said to the waitress, "You got to show folks some respect, sister. That ain't no way to be speaking to nobody." While the waitress and the man argued, I felt sad for both of them. I could understand how they both felt. I said to my mom, "Everyone, even the homeless street person, needs to feel respected."

Another way you can show respect for others is to avoid interrupting when someone is speaking. If you want to speak to someone and they are already talking to another person, you should say "Excuse me." After that, you need to wait to be acknowledged before you begin talking. You should not just walk up to another person and begin your own conversation when others are talking.

My parents have taught that every human being needs to feel respected, even the homeless. We must take a person's feelings, needs, and thoughts into consideration. When people respect one another there are fewer arguments. Therefore, treat others the way you want to be treated and you will have no problem earning respect. You will simply feel better about yourself when you show respect. Therefore, respect is the law of life I want to follow and I hope you do too.

THERE'S NO RACISM IN RESPECT

Anonymous, 5th Grade

It was my first day in third grade at Franklin School in South Plainfield. It was a beautiful afternoon. I was on my way to recess after lunch. A boy, not of my skin color, was holding the door for people. When I got to the door, he shut it and ran to play. I didn't know why he didn't hold the door for me. Then I realized why, because I was 1 out of 10 blacks in that school. I felt so mad. I felt mad because I thought black and white people were equal. I also felt an empty space in my heart. Right then I felt racism around me. When recess was over I went over to the boy who hadn't held the door. I said, "Why didn't you hold the door for me?" He replied, "I can't talk to you." Even after what he did and said, I still had respect for him. Dr. Martin Luther King, Jr. always said to treat people the way you want to be treated. But in this situation, the boy treated me the way he didn't want to be treated.

To me, respect means having appreciation for yourself, family, and your environment. I still think about what happened in 3rd grade. I also think about what Dr. King and other black heroes went through to make it possible for whites and blacks to sit at the table of sister- and brotherhood, go to the same school, drink at the same water fountains, be together in the same places, and work together as a nation. *Laws of Life* are the values by which people live. My *Law of Life* is respect. I believe you need to have respect for everyone no matter skin color or background. Respect comes to mind whenever someone treats me bad and makes me angry. I let God deal with the things they do because hate in my heart will consume me too. So, I promise to respect people no matter what they are or what they do.

OPENING MY HEART

Anonymous, 5th Grade

My law of life is respect. I think it is a great thing for all people. When I become a parent, I would like to demonstrate respect to my children. Children have to learn how to be respectful to other people and to themselves.

When I was seven years old, I didn't have respect because I thought that my family didn't respect me. I didn't care about anything or anybody. Years have passed and I realize that I do care about people and those people are my family. They are the ones who give me love and they are the ones who care about me. Even if sometimes they aren't perfect, they are still my family and I am proud of that. I am proud that I have a family who knows how to respect others and I am proud that my family shows me the things they know. Sometimes I wonder how it would be if I was an adult. I know that when I become an adult I am going to have a family. It is going to be up to me to take care of them and I am going to show them what my family has shown me about having respect for others.

A personal experience that developed my law of life happened when I was in El Salvador. My aunt was taking care of me because my mom was working in the United States. My mother couldn't take care of me while she was working, so she sent me to live in El Salvador. I was a bad kid and I never listened to my aunt. I didn't care about what other people said about me and I always got mad when my aunt said to clean up my room. I didn't have respect for people. When I was in El Salvador I thought that having fun was the best thing in life, but I now know that having fun is not the best part of life. Sometimes you have to go through hard times because you could learn from them. The only way I learned this was after my great-grandfather died. I felt so sad that I wanted to go to heaven with him. I missed him so much because he meant the world to me and we used to have a lot of fun. He was the person who set an example for me. He told me that, with a little bit of respect, we could all go a long way. He was the person I really loved and the only person that I showed love to. From this I learned that even if a person who you love passes away, life still goes on. We are left with the lessons they have taught us. That day was the saddest day of my life. That was the day I did everything my aunt told me to do. That was the day I opened my heart to my family. My mind started opening, too. Even if I missed my great-grandfather, I still had to keep living.

A world event that has helped me to develop my law of life was when Osama Bin Laden attacked the Twin Towers. I think he lacked respect for life because he killed many people. I learned that he wanted a war with the United

States. But what does war do? It doesn't do anything but bring hatred, and hatred brings more war. I think the terrorists were jealous of the United States. Every country knows that when they hit the Twin Towers they broke the hearts of a lot of people. I think everything has changed since then. Every person knows that the United States will protect its freedom and that those who attack us have to respect the property that belongs to us. We are human beings and we have to be treated that way. We want to be treated with respect. What they did was a terrible thing. I will never forget September, 11, 2001 because that was the day when families were destroyed and people were left homeless. After that day, I learned that respect for life is the key for all people who want freedom.

Chapter Four

Perseverance

MY PRE- AND POST-PERSEVERANCE LIFE

Dr. Larry Leverett, Executive Director, Panasonic Foundation and Former Superintendent of Plainfield Public Schools

Many of us have heard the adage, "You can't judge a book by its cover." I have read hundreds of books, and have to admit that sometimes I chose a particular title based on the attractiveness of the cover. But, over the years, I have learned that there is much more to know about a book than the cover can tell you. What people may see and judge from the "cover" fails to tell the complete story.

Many people may look at the 'cover' of my life and judge me to be a successful person. They may point to my advanced degrees in education, a career that has included gubernatorial appointments to commissions and boards and, more recently, by the First Lady of the United States. They may have read articles I have written, heard speeches I have delivered, or seen television shows on which I have appeared. Some would conclude that my life has been marked by goal attainment and personal and professional fulfillment. My life's "cover" may communicate to the outsider the façade of an accomplished, confident and self-assured person who sets goals and gets the job done. Some of this may be true, however, the road I have traveled is far more complicated than what appears to be the case. The reality is that struggle, hardship, and failures in my personal and professional life have littered the road to my present existence. My success is due to perseverance.

I like to read and recall, "Your Blues Ain't Like Mine," written by Bebe Moore Campbell, an African American author. In that work, Ms. Campbell taught a powerful life lesson, one I draw upon continuously. Regardless of our life circumstances, we all will have some "Blues" in our lives. We may communicate one thing to the outside world, but we all struggle internally, we all contend with difficulties as we attempt to figure out the kind of person we want to become. We all have our own special variation of the "Blues" being played inside us, and it may not be identifiable to those looking at our lives from the outside. The decisions we make about how to deal with our "Blues" shape the direction of our lives in many important ways.

One important element of my struggles has been perseverance. I take this to be one of my main Laws of Life. If truth be told, I can separate my life into two distinct parts: Pre-perseverance and Post- perseverance.

The pre-perseverance part was a time when I didn't manage my "Blues" very well. It was a time when I accepted failure, could not summon up the energy to work toward achieving goals, believed that my fate was pre-determined and there was little I could do to alter the direction my life would go. I recall sitting in high school and college classrooms experiencing a great deal of difficulty learning. In several instances, I just plain gave up and cut class, spent no time studying, didn't complete assignments and just accepted the fact that I would fail. In my sophomore year, things got so bad that I was placed on academic probation. I simply did not see myself working hard and having faith and confidence in my ability to be a successful student. This lack of perseverance was also evident in other parts of my life. I had allowed myself to rationalize my trials in ways that placed the blame on others. I accepted little responsibility for doing what I could to change my situation.

Fortunately, this pre-Perseverance phase was not fatal and I somehow managed to return to the lessons taught by my parents, grandparents, Sunday school teachers, and school teachers, all of whom saw a better life for me. I had been taught that hard work and belief in oneself and God were important qualities necessary to have a good and meaningful life. I recall the many times when my Mom, Etta Mae, encouraged me to persevere in spite of hardship and challenge. It is these lessons that I now draw upon as I live each day. Perseverance has become a key value, one that I incorporate it into all aspects of my life. I call my present life the post-perseverance phase, life as it looks after one is able to accept defeat and failure as part of one's regular diet. Developing habits of persevering has made me a much more capable and fulfilled person. They shape my life decisions. "Blues" continue to be a large part of my reality, but I now have the faith and confidence that allow me to persist when trouble comes my way.

To persevere has required that I reach deeply into my inner self and first summon up the commitment to stare failure or defeat in the face, then find the motivation to challenge what I had accepted as the inevitability of failure. For

me, faith has become a giant resource. Faith is one of the keys to perseverance. In her last will and testament, Mary McCloud Bethune shared this wisdom: "With faith, all things are possible, without faith nothing is possible."
Faith provides a source of spiritual and moral nourishment. It allows us to believe that things can be better or different. Faith in God and in oneself can fuel
us through hard times. Without it, it is hard to maintain a sense of optimism
about our ability to make a difference. When the "faith gauge" is near empty,
it is difficult to put forth the effort to overcome obstacles. Keeping mine full
by paying regular attention to my spiritual state has proven to be vital to confronting difficulty successfully. A second law might be maintaining a strong
sense of personal efficacy. When we are efficacious, we are invested in making a difference. We set goals that are important to us, work hard to achieve
them, and do not accept defeat. If you don't believe you can make a difference, it is unlikely that you can summon up the spirit necessary to overcome
difficult circumstances.

Looking back on my life, I am thankful for the early lesson of perseverance. It provided the foundation for me to get beyond merely accepting my
life's "Blues" as fate. As a law of life, perseverance is deeply embedded into
all aspects of my being. No longer do I choose to wallow in sad acceptance
of whatever life deals out. Instead, I persevere, strive, work through challenges, do what ever it takes to be a good person, an accomplished educator,
and a spiritually and emotionally happy person. I also offer no alibis or ex-
cuses to explain away failure. And, lastly, I believe I can make a difference
and through faith, hard work and confidence in myself and others, I persevere.

LIFE'S JOURNEY

Anonymous, 11th Grade

Growing up in Plainfield, I'd have to admit that many of the citizens and those
who have grown up along side me have fallen victim to the various stereotypes
put upon people of our specific social status. So many simply succumb to the
pressures and hardships of this unpredictable life. However seeing these cir-
cumventable mistakes made by those who were the most influential in my earlier years, I realized that I don't want to end up like the thousands who forcibly
forfeited their opportunity to further their education at an institution of higher
learning, so as to be able to fend for both their families and themselves. Ambition, wisdom, and perseverance are the key weapons equipping me for this

life long journey. Although these are not the only laws that I abide by, they are the most essential to me as concerns my future.

Determination, willingness to work hard, putting my future into perspective (becoming a lawyer and psychologist), and going full force into life are necessary if I want to attain both happiness and success. Ambition, my first law of life is what is needed the most. It is like the gasoline in an automobile, it fuels it all and allows others to function, too. My ambition is my constant push/desire to do or be more. Because of it, I can take each experience for what it is worth, drive straight past all opposition and head directly down the road to my prize.

Gained through multiple trial and error experiences, wisdom is my next law of life. Taking into account lessons learned either by myself or through the advice of those who may have already gone along this path, my journey will be made much easier because I will have knowledge of what may come. Knowledgeable peers or adults may offer advice based on their life experiences but, the best lessons are those I will learn through making my own mistakes. Since I am an assertive and courageous person who is not willing to always to seek guidance before acting, like a baby discovering fire for the first time, I will get no doubt burned and gain from an unforgettable lesson. It is through events like this that I expect to gain wisdom along the way.

Ambition initiates things, wisdom comes later. I know that success is not something that can be achieved over night. Patience is truly a virtue. It may take a while for me to reach my final stage of success. Trouble can only last for so long. Maintaining a level head and keeping everything in perspective and manageable, will make it possible to endure this storm. In fact, it will be a mere bump in the road. So, my final law of life is perseverance.

Watching so many members of my family settle for pennies when they could be worth millions is saddening. They have yet to achieve any level of true happiness, yet they remain content with their living conditions. However, the combination of these laws of life gives me a secret weapon and enables me confront every obstacle with ease.

PERSEVERANCE: THE KEY TO SUCCESS

Eddie Brack, 8th Grade

Everyday begins with a new struggle, whether it is a crisis at home, or the work of overcoming fear of failure at school. Some people are the victims of bullying; others have to deal with peer pressure. Sometimes you have to be courageous, other times you must be able to love. I believe every being on earth faces problems and every one of them lives by different laws of life to solve them. The key to success in my life is perseverance. My purpose is to continue to reach my goals, despite difficulties that I may face.

I live in an urban community, one that has many drawbacks, there is a huge amount of drug activity and gang violence. The people in my community have greatly influenced me to strive harder because I don't want to end up like some of them. The people that persevere in life are some of the many that influence my decisions. My great grandmother was a person who struggled to make sure her family would be successful. Born in 1902, she was a maid who worked extremely hard just to make ends meet. She walked miles to get to work because she didn't have money for transportation; after working in someone's kitchen all day, she came home to take in laundry. Her driving desire to make life better for her children and theirs motivated her to persevere in a time when being black meant you were considered less than nothing.

My cousin was a product of a drug addicted mother; she left him in the hospital because her need for drugs overpowered her need to be a parent. He was adopted by my aunt and has faced many health problems as well as learning disabilities. His parents stood by his side through the many surgeries he needed to correct the problems resulting from his mother's drug use. The man he knows as his father died, and his mother is very sickly. The many tragedies he has suffered have caused him to realize that he must persevere to rise above his birth. His parents have made many sacrifices in order to give him the opportunity to have a better life.

My motivation to persevere drives me to show my family that I can and will be successful. I want to set a precedent of high achievement so my family doesn't end up with nothing. My family may fuss at me, but they do this only because they want and expect the best of me. I always hear people say that as black males we will end up in jail, on the street corner or dead. Society already expects less from me, so I feel as if I have to give more, to break away from being in any of those categories. Maybe I can influence my peers to keep their heads up when life gets hard.

Models of perseverance are all around us. Martin Luther King Jr., Malcolm X, and Rosa Parks are a few of the people that made it possible for me to write this essay. These people led by example and they persevered through adversity. They also never wavered in their commitment to bring about positive change. I think living my life by the laws of perseverance will determine how well my future turns out.

NEVER GIVE UP

Anonymous, 8th Grade

Out of all the different laws of life, "Never give up," means the most to me. I love my mother very much because she taught me this. If you give up, you will never succeed at anything. Everyday of my life, I struggle to "never give up" because I plan to be a doctor.

My mother was a good student in elementary school, junior high school, and up to high school. When she was in high school her parents divorced. She had seven younger brothers and sisters she had to help care for. Her mother was very sick, and in and out of the hospital. Her father left home, but she "never gave up."

My mother was planning to graduate from high school and go to college just like her parents, and older sister and brother. She had a guidance counselor who refused to put her in the honors math classes for two years. She knew something was wrong, but with no one to help her, she became discouraged, she graduated from high school, but she gave up wanting to attend college.

Twenty years later when she was older, my mother thought about college again. A trip to Africa helped her see that she was wasting time. A friend told her that if she still wanted to go to college, it was not too late. She was very afraid, but she went to college anyway.

My mom excelled and kept a 4.0 grade average. She was elected president of Phi Theta Kappa, the honor society. She traveled all over America with Phi Theta Kappa. After three years, she graduated valedictorian of her class, and got a scholarship to Columbia University. She is so happy she "never gave up."

Before graduating, she was in a very bad car accident that burst her heart. For a year she walked around feeling weak, not knowing what was wrong. She was admitted to the hospital multiple times, but no one helped her. She "never gave up" and kept going to work and school. She went to the doctor at Columbia, and he told her she needed heart surgery immediately or she could die.

My mom had to stop going to Columbia to have surgery. She felt very bad and she felt like another obstacle was being put in her way, but she "did not give up." Even when she was sick and injured, she "never gives up." Every day she tells me to keep working hard to achieve my dream of becoming a doctor. She also says that, if she had kept going after high school, she would be doing much better.

My mother almost gave up her dream years ago and she waited a long time to try again. Now she says she will "never give up." To this day, she continues to be a role model in my life, because she continues to show me why I should "never give up."

JUST KEEP TRYING

Anonymous, 5th Grade

Have you ever tried and tried to do something, but kept getting frustrated because you couldn't get it right? Have you wanted to give up trying, but then didn't? I have. When you don't give up easily when working at a hard task, you show perseverance. Perseverance means sticking to a purpose or an aim, never giving up what you have set out to do. It has affected my life greatly. Last summer, my camp was planning a trip to an indoor ice skating rink. I didn't want to go because I didn't know how to skate. I asked my mom if I could stay home on the day of the trip. I explained why. She said, "The only way to learn how to do something is to try it and keep trying until you finally get it."

The day of the trip arrived. Everyone was excited but me. As we got to the rink, I felt nervous. I was the only one there who didn't already know how to skate. When I stepped onto the ice it felt slippery. I almost fell. If I had fallen, I would have become embarrassed, so I sat out for most of the time.

While I was sitting, watching everyone else skate, I remembered what my mom had said about trying until you finally accomplish what you want. I decided to try again. I stepped onto the ice and tried and tried. I kept falling. I got frustrated. I thought about giving up, but forced myself to keep skating. I thought I'd never learn how. I continued falling, hurting my arms and legs. I started to cry because I was so frustrated. I really wanted to be able to skate. Finally, I tried again. I was so determined, and angry that, guess what? I didn't realize it but I was skating. I learned how to skate because of the effort I made and because I followed my mom's advice. I felt glad and proud because I had stuck to my purpose and hadn't given up. If I had not persevered, I wouldn't have learned how to skate. As I grow up, I'll continue to follow my mom's advice, and never give up on what I set out to do. I will become a success because I know how to persevere!

LEARNING TO SUCCEED

Dorel Simmons, 5th Grade

I almost failed the first, second, third and fourth grades because I was not doing my class work or my homework and did not always listen to the teacher. Even though many people thought that I wasn't trying hard enough, and I must admit that sometimes that was the truth. Still, I never gave up. I kept on trying.

At the end of the second marking period in my fourth grade year, I met a new teacher in the Resource Room. She told me that I could be anything that I wanted to be as long as I put my mind to it. To prevent me from falling asleep, which I always did, she would send me to wash my face and count to three until I returned to the class. My teacher believed in me even when I did not believe in myself. I remember telling her how much I hated to write, but she would always tell me that I have to in order to get through life. The first time I completed a report I felt so good. My dad, mom, and even the principal of our school came and looked at it. I felt very successful because I had completed an assignment. It made me realize that I could do anything; I just had to believe in myself.

I remember when I first met my fifth grade teacher. She made me feel hopeful because she told my dad that she would do whatever she could to help me make it through the fifth grade. I also told myself that I would ignore anyone who tried to distract me because I am going to make it. Even though this is not easy, I am trying my best. I have come to realize that whatever I do now in life will determine how successful I'll be when I grow up. When I am in the Resource Room and when I am with my fifth grade class my goal is to complete all my assignments. I feel extremely happy when I look around the Resource Room and see my work posted. I feel like a winner!

Even though I was not a bright student in my early school career, I am experiencing success now. It is fantastic and I know that I am going to make it. My law of life is that I will never give up on myself and I am going to do whatever it takes to complete my education, so that when I graduate I will become a very successful electrician just like my dad.

"HE WHO FALLS TODAY MAY RISE TOMORROW"

Liz Colocho, 5th Grade

For a long time, my life was full of constant changes. When I was born, my whole family was together. But, by the time my second birthday arrived, we lived in separate places. My Papi left first when I was only one year old. He wanted the best for me and my brother Javier. In our country, El Salvador, he wasn't able to make enough money for us to live on. He went to America to look for a better job and promised to send for us as soon as he could. After a few months, my Mommi decided to go to America and help my Father. My brother and I went to live with one of my Uncles and his wife. On the exact day of my second birthday in 1992, my brother also went to America to be with my parents. I could not go with him because they didn't have enough money to send for both of us.

After my brother left, my Abuela, my mother's mother, took me home with her. I was closer to my Niamalita, my Father's mother, but I didn't get a vote. Several years later, right before Christmas, my Abuela died. I felt very lonely and sad especially because I couldn't remember my parent's faces and wondered if they had forgotten about me. I wondered what would happen to me. "I want to see my parents!" my heart shouted. After my grandmother died I lived with my Aunt and cousins. I was lucky to have them. They gave me everything I wanted but they couldn't give me the love I wanted from my parents.

I still remember the day my Mommi wrote that she was sending for me to come to America. I was very happy because I was finally going to have the family, parents and brother, I always wanted all seven years of my life.

This experience taught me that sometimes parents have to make decisions, choices that children don't understand. I've learned that sometimes in life you will experience hardships, pain, and disappointment. But, experience helps us to learn that life can be full of uncertainties and it also helps us to make decisions about how we want to live our lives. Pam Mufloz wrote in her book *Esperanza Rising* "He who falls today may rise tomorrow." My life experiences have taught me that just because there may be pitfalls in life it doesn't mean that you can't get up and start all over again.

Chapter Five

Love

WHO TAUGHT YOU ABOUT LOVE?

Maurice J. Elias

> *"Love given is love received."* —*John Marks Templeton*
> *"The more love we give, the more love we have left."*—*John Marks Templeton*

Did you even stop to think about who taught you what you know about love? Thanks to the *Laws of Life* Essay, I had a chance to do just that. Three people taught me a lot about love: my Nona (my mother's mother), my older daughter Sara Elizabeth, and my younger daughter, Samara Alexandra. They all taught me the same basic message, the more love you give, the more love you will receive. They also taught me an important related message: Love is not merely reciprocal.

My Nona loved me very much. When I was born, my parents and I lived in her apartment in the Bronx. The neighborhood was urban and very ethnically mixed. Our apartment was right next to the elevated train line, but I got used to the noise in a short time. We were there until I was 7, when we moved to Queens. Nona moved near us pretty soon thereafter, until she passed away when I was about 15 years old.

I knew she loved me because she always smiled when she saw me. We laughed together when she watched Merv Griffin on television, even though I was pretty sure she didn't understand most of it. She never really learned to write English and didn't read very well, but she always seemed excited to read anything I showed her. Most of all, she loved to bake for me. She used to make bourekias (Greek pastries with cheese or spinach) and roskas (a slightly sweet small roll). She used to let me help and, of course, taste the ingredients along the way. And she used to let me taste them as soon as they came out of the oven, when they were the best. She didn't worry about spoiling my appetite, she didn't worry that my helping might ruin her recipe, and she didn't worry when I spilled some flour or egg or grated cheese. As I got older and spent less time with her, none of these things seemed to matter to her. Whenever I came over, it was always the same, even when she was feeling more and more ill. Her love for me was not based on the expectation that I would reciprocate.

My daughter Sara taught me about love when she was born. I didn't know what kind of parent I would be or how I would relate to an infant. I saw Sara come into the world and I got to give her her very first bath. From the first time she looked up at me, I was filled with a powerful feeling of a kind I never felt before. It was caring, sharing, warmth, importance, responsibility, and tremendous joy all wrapped up into one. The feeling was love. And all I had to do to feel it was spend time with Sara, hold her, read to her, play with her, even change her diaper. The more love I showed to her, the more love I got back in return. Sara is now 27, and these feelings are still strong today.

And the same is also true for Samara. After Sara was born, I wasn't sure I had enough love in me to share with two children. I was worried about not being able to be a loving father to a second child. But when Samara was born, I found still stronger feelings of love that I didn't know I had. And, the more I cared for Samara and did things with her, the more love I felt. She adored her big sister and especially liked the things we did together as a family. Her happiness was contagious, and her greatest joy growing up was singing. Samara was in various vocal groups, including the New Jersey All-State Choir. When she sang, she was filled with tremendous pride and satisfaction. I had the same feelings just listening to her. Sharing moments of accomplishment and joy like these with Samara, as well as Sara, has always deepened my feelings of love and affection for both of them. And these feelings on my part were never diminished when we had curfew conflicts or when they didn't remember to clean their rooms or do their homework. Love is not merely reciprocal.

When children don't have love in their lives, they are missing something, like having a chocolate ice cream sundae without any chocolate. It's just not the same. But Sara and Samara taught me that you never know when love will strike you and you never know when your own capacity for love will be deepened. It's never too late to extend your love and caring to others, to help them feel loved even when they may seem, or feel, unlovable. By loving those who need more love in their lives, you will help them – and also do a lot for yourself. As my Nona taught me, the more love you give, the more love you receive. But as she and her grandchildren taught me also, love is not merely reciprocal. When you give love to get it, you are bound to be disappointed. When you give love out of a genuine sense of care, you'll find the love coming back to you in abundance. This is why Love is one of my most important *Laws of Life*.

ONE REASON I AM HERE IS TO GIVE AND RECEIVE LOVE

Danielle Sterling, 11th Grade

As young girl, I was taught that everyone on this earth had a purpose. Many times, I have often wondered what mine was. However, now that I am crossing over to adulthood, I realize why God has placed me on this Earth. Yet, that cannot just be summed up in one word. Love, determination, and religion are just few of the words that come to mind when I think of this. Because I have a many-sided personality, I think that I have many purposes on this earth. In brief, God gave me a reason for being here.

To most people, love is just a feeling. Although that is true, love is much more than how one person feels. This one particular feeling can describe how one not only feels about themselves, but also how others feel. One of my main purposes in this world is to not only love, but also to be loved. The unconditional love that I give and receive from those who I care about always reminds me of why I am here. I especially am reminded of this when I think of my mother. She has been my purpose for all of my life. The love that we have for each other is greater than anything one can imagine. Being that I am an only child and that she is a single mother, our connection is stronger than the average mother-daughter relationship. Time and again, we have stuck together to overcome the obstacles that were ahead of us. In brief, love is one of the many reasons that I was placed here.

At a young age, I knew that I loved music. I loved everything from the lyrics to the melody. I knew that music was my passion. And since then, I have realized that music was one of my many purposes in life. Though, I have been unsure of what I really wanted to do, I know that music has to be a part of me where ever I go. Therefore I have to work hard and be determined in order to pursue a career in music. Determination is not only the key to success, but it is also one of the only ways that I can do what I love. However, I am not only determined to pursue music, I am also determined to do my best in everyday life. My purpose is to work hard to reach my goal not only for myself, but also for those who may consider me a role model.

I have always believed that God is the most important force in my life. Without Him, none of my blessings and good fortune would be possible. Therefore, I know that one of the reasons that God has placed me here is to praise, honor, and love Him. With God in my life, I can defeat all challenges that may come my way. He also gives me the strength to stay away from evil temptation and overcome peer pressure. God has walked with me through the hardships that I have faced in the past, and I know that He will be there in the future. That is why I not only make it my purpose, but also my mission to love honor and respect the Lord.

In conclusion, it is obvious that I have many purposes for being here. I am here first and foremost to love and honor God and be thankful to Him for his many blessings. I am also here to give and receive unconditional love from those who I care about the most. Lastly, I am here to work hard to reach all the goals that I have set for myself. These three factors define who I am today. Without these, I do not think that I would understand my place in this world. Yet, with these I realize and understand that my place in this world may affect the lives of many.

LOVE IS EVERYWHERE

Anonymous, 11th Grade

Love can reach so many levels, particularly love for people, such as family, friends, or for the person you want to spend the rest of your life with. When we are children, all we understand is the simple truth that when someone said they loved you, you felt special and needed. But as we grow older the definition gets extremely confusing for some, because not everything is so black and white anymore. Love does not only involve how people feel about other people, but how we feel about almost everything else. The love of nature, the love of life and of creation, all of it. People are faced with choices they never dreamed of, and that is why my law of life is love.

When I was very young, I developed a love of all kinds of music and inherited that love from my parents. I grew up listening to almost everything ranging from r&b, salsa, country, gospel, and many other genres of music. It seems that whatever kind of music I was listening to, everyone was talking about love. Lyrics about how love had shaken their hearts, or about how people can't wait to fall in love, or about what they would do for the person they loved and various others. As I grew older, listening to music stopped being about singing along with the artist to some catchy tune. I began to actually interpret what the writers were saying. Sometimes I liked what the author was saying about love, and other times I didn't. No one wants to hear that you can get your heart broken by loving someone completely.

But I continued to dig deeper until I reached the roots. And, whether or not the lyrics I read were about the hardships in finding and keeping love, or letting it go, they always left me with the feeling of amazement. I would watch television and observe the many couples on various shows, as people put lyrics in motion. I saw couples in perfect bliss, and I saw the faces of the dejected. I would even watch how my own family related to each other, and I relished the thought of one day adding to the prevailing family unit. I tried to discover why this intriguing thing called love could make people go to such amazing lengths for one another. I watched hearts being broken and relationships shattered, but yet still people were destined to fall in love. With love comes amazing things like the feeling of belonging. But with the good comes the bad and not everything can always be sunshine and roses.

I believe love can begin to resemble a kaleidoscope—every choice one makes regarding it can change everything. Love is the driving force of our lives. It fuels us to succeed, to be more than content with what we have. If we lived without love, no one would be moved to do anything worthwhile. What a sad world that would be. If we could live without love, then maybe we would all know some peace, but or lives would be hollow. And with that hollowness, who could possibly be happy? To love is to sacrifice, whether we want to or not. We learn to adapt to situations just so we can stay in love.

The lyrics "The Greatest Thing You'll Ever Learn, Is Just To Love, And Be Loved In Return" were written by Eden Ahbez. They words that I have absorbed over the years when they were sung by various artists. The artist may have changed, but the significance always remains the same. Even though there are many lessons in life, none are greater then experiencing what love has to offer.

To know love is simply to live life. With all that surrounds us, beyond all the fear of being alone in this crazy world, there is still the security of knowing that love is always right around the corner, in the form of something wondrous. In the end, all we have to do is seek it out.

AMOR

Jose A. Gonzollez, 8th Grade

El amor es una corta y sencilla palabra pero, con un gran significado, el amor es el sentimiento que une a las personas, es el respeto que se tiene uno mismo, el amor lo es todo.

El amor es, el sacrificio que nuestros padres hacen dia a dia para ir a tra-
bajar y poder brindarnos lo que nesecitamos. El amor es el apoyo que ellos
nos dan cada dia, es el regano y castigo que nos dan al nosotros fallarles. El
amor es aquel orgullo que nosotros sentimos hacia nuestros padres, es el
poder decir. "El senor y la senora que estan ahi son mis padres."

El amor, el amor es la humillacion que Dios vivio al venir a este mundo y
dar la vida por cada uno de nosotros, el derramar su sangre en una cruz por
nosotros. El amor es el deseo y la nesecidad de brindar nuestra ayuda a los
demas, es el poder compartir lo que tenemos con los demas. Es la atraccion y
empeno por salir adelante, el poder ver el futuro, el tener la sporrans de que
un dia recibiremos la recompensa de lo que somos o hemos hecho. El amor
es lo que nos da el poder para enfrentarnos a los obstacles y problemas que
tenemos en la vida.

El amor, el amor lo es todo, es tu vida, tu sporrans, tus fuerzas y tu necesi-
dad. Con el amor logras y realizes todo loque te propones. Es lo que te ayuda
a vivir, a existir, lo que te da el valor para sobresalir y darte conocer en la
vida, es la serenaded y patience que tienes para decir que no a lo malo, a se
parar te de coquilles que dicen ser tus amigos y lo unico que quieren el elle-
vart a la perdicion. Eso es, es simplemente, el "AMOR."

THE SHOW AND TELL OF LOVE

Keba Smith, 8th Grade

Love is a strong act of devotion to something or someone. It is a great feeling of knowing you can wake up and go to sleep knowing someone loves you.
Love has the power to bring about weddings, dates, and even the birth of a
child. It is the special feeling that you can't help but enjoy.

Love is an emotion that has two parts, show and tell. The show part is the
hugs, kisses, jewelry, cards, flowers, candy and stuffed animals given out to
many people daily. The tell part is the "I love you" which is said or written in
poems and letters written by many people.

The love between my mother and I is more of a show and not tell. From
when I wake up in the morning, to when I go to sleep at night, she is always
giving me love. When I wake up I always get a hug. When I'm hungry I always have a full meal and when I go to sleep, I get tucked in with a kiss on
the forehead.

My father and I have the tell part of love. Even if we may not live together, he tries his best to make sure I know he loves me. My dad calls and sends cards on every special holiday. The thing that says he loves me the most is that when we are on the phone he won't hang up without saying I love you. Those three words are also on every card I have.

I also express my feelings as the show and tell part of love. I show and tell both my mother and father love. I give back hugs and kisses and I write cards on every holiday that is most important to us. I also try buying presents when I can. Mostly, I try to be appreciative and I'm willing to give a helping hand.

Love is used in a good way, but it is also abused. People abuse love and hurt a lot of feelings. The most common way love is abused is to get money. People pry their way into other people's hearts and then break it in a split second. This is what is called negative and cold-hearted love. It is used to kill the spirits of other goodhearted people. These goodhearted people are the people who love, care and appreciate each other's feelings.

Love is the most special and valued emotion. It is important because life can't be lived without it. Love can't be lived without IT, because it is the trust that unites friends. Love is passion that holds together a couple and it is the relationship between a parent and a child.

The joy of love is that it can never go away. You can deny it, you can ignore it, and you can be negative to it. Love will always stay. Some people explain love as life and some explain it as another part of life that is lived. No matter how it is explained and by whom, love will be a joy and will forever stay. Love is special and shall forever be remembered and kept in the heart.

AMOR Y RESPETO

Ana Krawetz, 8th Grade

Amor y respeto. Fueron dos cosas por la cual en estos 13 anos de vida, he aprendido. Muchas personas piensan que el amor es tener un sentimiento por un muchacho o una muchacha, pero no es asi. El respeto puede ser que no lo sepa pronounce bien, pero lo practico todos los dias.

Mi heroina, la persona en que siento un gran carino y que hace 6 anos se murio, fue quien me enseno la palabra amor. Mia amigos y amigas piensan que el amor es un sentimiento por un muchacho o muchacha, pero no es asi.

Hace muchos anos por lo cual nunca olvidare, mi abuelita me dejo marcado en mi corazon lo que es el amor.

Yo me habia vestido de Santa Claus. Era la ultima Navidad que pasaria con ella. Por la noche toque a la puerta, mi abuela, con sus flacas piernas, abrio. Yo di los regales y todo habia pasado. Cuando en la manana sanguine, me desperto con una voz dulce mi angelito. Ella se sento a mi lado a hablarme de lo cuanto sintio que yo no estuviera alli donde "Santa Claus" estaba dando regales.

Con sus simples manos de trabajadora y con arthritis, mi abuela abrio una cajita donde adentro se encontraba un riquizimo dulce de guayaba. Ella me decia que como perdi los regales de "Santa Claus" porque estaba dormida, era para que yo comiera el dulce de guayaba, para endulsarme la vida.

Despues que probe estos dulces, le mire a sus lindos hojos color miel, sentia una paz enorme. A mi me Escanaba los dulces.

Un dia antes de que ella se muriera, hablamos por telefono. Ella me dijo que si algun dia ella fuera al cielo ella me hiba hacer un monton de dulces de guayaba. Hoy me pregunto, porque en este dia no le dije, "Abuelita te amo."

Ella me enseno tambien el respeto con las personas. Cada dia me decia con su caloroso abrazo, la importance del respeto. Una vez nos sentamos en el medio de la plantacio de hierbas naturals y me conto una pequena leyenda del respeto.

Esa leyenda hablaba de una nina que no respetaba a sus padres. Un dia ella necesito de sus padres, ya que se callo en un pozo profundo. Las unicas palabras que decia eran "Quiero a mi Mama~" Un hombre la escucho y le dijo, "Porque quieres a tu Mama ahora si no la respetas?"

Mi abuela me enseno a respetar al projimo y despues que la perdi, se lo cuanto que la amo. Una frase que llevo en mi corazon es que uno solo aprecia y extrana algo cuando lo pierde.

SOMETIMES YOU LOSE WHAT YOU LOVE THE MOST

Katheryne Rodriguez, 5th Grade

How do you spend time with your grandmother? When my grandma was alive we had the best times together. I called her Abuelita, which means grandma in Spanish. Abuelita and I loved to play with each other. Our favorite game was "I Spy," but we called it "Veo, veo."

One day when I came home from school, my mom told me we had to go to the doctor to take Abuelita because she was sick. When we got to the doctor's office, my mom told my brother and me to sit in the waiting room. Later on, when my mom came out, I asked her how Abuelita was doing. She told me that they found something in Abuelita's lower body, and if they had not taken it out it would have gotten worse. From that day on we went to see the doctor every week.

When we came home one day from the doctor, my mom said that Abuelita had lung cancer. As soon as she said that, all things flowed through my head. I remembered all the times we played together. I asked my mom if we could still play together like we used to. She said sure, but you just can't jump around with her anymore. Abuelita and I still played together, but we played quietly like walking in the garden or swinging in the maca (hammock). Sometimes when Abuelita felt like it, we would walk around the block and look at the flowers. Abuelita had lung cancer, so we had to be careful and go slow.

Abuelita went to Puerto Rico with my two aunts. A few weeks later when Abuelita came back, she became very, very sick. She became so sick that she called me girl, instead of my name. We had to take Abuelita to the hospital. One day when I was cleaning my messy room, my aunt came and told my mom that my cousin was having a birthday party and we were invited. My mom said we could go, so we got ready and went with my aunt. It was a long drive, but we were patient.

At the party I had a feeling Abuelita was not well. After the party was over we went home. There were a lot of cars parked by our house. When I got inside everybody was crying, and when I saw them I did not feel well. My mom told me that Abuelita had passed away. After she told me that, I was shocked and could not believe it. I went upstairs, my aunt hugged me and told me the story. She told me that before Abuelita died, she said she loved everybody. Then she took a deep breath and died with a smile on her face.

A few days later we went to the funeral and all my family and friends were there. When I was ready to do my speech, I couldn't do it. My aunt said it was all right and she went up to help me. Even though Abuelita, my grandma, is not here today, I will always remember her in my heart.

THE LOVE OF A TOTAL STRANGER

Adiyah Johnson, 5th Grade

Has anyone ever helped you in your time of need? I have had the experience of a stranger entering into my life and showing me love. About eighteen months ago, my mom got into some really bad trouble with the law, and she needed someone to take care of my two sisters and me.

At that time, while we were in the living room, there were a whole lot of police officers in our house. The police told my mom that she could only make three phone calls. She made two calls, but she didn't reach anyone. Her last phone call was to her friend's mother whom I had never met.

They lady had only five minutes to get to our house or the police were going to call DYFS [NJ Division of Youth and Family Services, the agency that follows up any charges of child maltreatment and that has the responsibility of child protection]. She came immediately. When she got there, my sisters and I were very scared. She said, "Don't worry, everything will be okay." She took us to her car and we all drove off. I had no idea where we were going. Therefore, I sat quietly in the car. She drove us around the corner to her house. When we went inside she tried to calm us down.

Later that evening, she made some phone calls. First she called my aunt to let her know what happened. She left three messages, but my aunt never returned her calls. She then realized that she had three little girls to take care of. Fortunately, we stayed with her.

A month later, she got legal custody of us. We still had not heard from our own family members, but I didn't worry about it because I was having fun. Since we've come to our new home, a lot of new and exciting things have been happening. We've been to Georgia with Ms. G., and we met her mom, grandmother, sister, and nephews. They all showed us much love. Even though our own flesh and blood relatives turned their backs on us when we needed them the most, God sent us a new family that loves us. We fit in with them because we love them too. Therefore, my law of life is about receiving love from a total stranger. She did make a difference in my life. I am thankful for everyday that I am given a chance to find love.

LOVING EVEN WHEN YOU LOSE SOMEONE

Rashaun Rawles, 5th Grade

Laws of Life are rules that I live my life by. I think loving others is the most important of them. A person must have love in his or her life. Love makes a person feel important. I had love in my life. That person died. She was my Aunt Pam.

On a cold, sunny morning I went to my aunt's house. She's my mother's sister. I loved her a lot and she loved me too. We were real cool. We always did a lot of fun things. Her kids are my favorite cousins. They come and visit my house just about every weekend. We play fun games, go on trips, and have lots of fun.

My Aunt Pam went to the hospital because she wasn't feeling well. My mom took her. I asked my aunt if she was going to be o.k. She said, "Yes, honey." I asked her, "When will you get out?" She replied, "When I feel better." "Are you getting out before my birthday?" I asked. My aunt said, "I hope so." She also said that when she got out of the hospital we were going to have a party. I told my aunt, "I love you!" She answered, "I love you, too!"

Aunt Pam was released from the hospital on a Thursday. Then the next day she cried, "I am not feeling so good." My mom took her to a different hospital. She was real sick. The doctors ran tests and called my house. They said something did not look right. My aunt had cancer. We were all furious that the first hospital did not find anything wrong. A week later the cancer had traveled through her body. She was still in the hospital on my birthday. Two days later she died. My whole family was sad. I was sad because the things we were planning on doing together we will never have a chance to do.

My aunt's love meant a lot to me because we were real close. Now she is looking down on me and saying, "Everything is o.k." I love my Aunt Pam. Rest in peace.

I am grateful that I had my aunt's love. Even though she has passed away. I will always cherish our special memories. I believe it is very important to love others. Loving others is a Law of Life that I wish for everyone.

MY MOM BELIEVES IN ME

Kimeisha Murphy, 5th Grade

Love is a deep feeling for someone that you are fond of. It is a special relationship of attachment between two people. It is the kind of feeling or affection that a mother and daughter share. It is the deep warm feeling that any parent feels for her child. Love is something that we should display everyday for everybody. I love my mother and we have a very special relationship. I would like for you to read and understand my special story on Love.

One day, I had to recite a part in our school's Black History play. I was really scared and excited at the same time. This was my first time in a school play and I wanted to do well. I had to recite and act the part of a famous leader, Harriet Tubman. My mother told me "Do your best and remember I will be sitting in the front." She told me that she was very proud of me and that she loves me. She told me that "I would give you a standing ovation" with a smile on her face and she will give me a surprise. As I was getting dressed in my silk purple African outfit, I felt butterflies in my stomach. I tried to get rid of them by thinking of happy things.

I was in the first grade and wanted to make my mother proud of me. My mother gave me a kiss before I went on the stage. As I began my part, I started to cry a little. I started to cry because everyone was laughing at me. I thought that they were all laughing at my outfit.

My teacher came on stage, I took a deep breath, my mother threw me a kiss and I recited my part like a professional. I got a standing ovation and the principal praised me at the end of the program. My mother was standing and smiling. She was so happy and proud of me. She told me softly "I love you." I felt really felt good about myself and my part in the play.

My butterflies were all gone and I was a star all that day at school. My mother's love and belief in me made it possible for me to survive. I remember her telling me that she loves me and that she did not want me to mess up.

I told my mom that I would do my best and she would be happy. My mother helped me practice a lot and I did not want to disappoint her. I was happy for what my mother said to me and for helping me with my part. I was happy because I did what I was supposed to and I got lots of compliments.

Our relationship was special and we always talk. This story was special to me because I remember that she said she believed in me and that made me feel special. That is why we have a special relationship and I can talk to her anytime and she can talk to me about anything. And, that is why I am sharing my special story about love.

SHOW LOVE ALL THE TIME

Albert McWilliams, 5th Grade

"Ahhh!" cried my mom. She was extremely sad. My grandfather had just passed away. My mom cried the whole night through. I knew my grandfather loved my mom more than life itself. It was time I showed my mom I loved her even more. I just had to cheer her up, I knew there was a way. That is when I learned the true meaning of love.

To me, love means lots of things. It means to have kindness and respect for all things, even if others have not showed the same to you. In the Bible, Paul states in Corinthians chapter thirteen, "I may be able to speak the language of men and even angels but if I have no love, my speech is no more than a noisy gong or a clanging bell."

To me Paul is saying, if someone has no love, everything he says would have no meaning. It also means if someone has no love, his or her life means nothing. Love is very special, it is a virtue that should be carried out through everyone's life.

In the Bible it also says, "Love is patient and kind.....It is not conceited, selfish or irritable."

To me love is endlessly important in life. Everyone should agree on this, love, no matter what his or her religious beliefs.

When my grandfather died, it was very hard to find a smile on my mother's face. It might have been hard but that did not stop me. I knew if I tried hard enough, I could do it. Every time I saw my mom I tried to make her laugh. Most of the time humor wasn't enough. When laughing did not work, I worked up my strength and gave her a humongous bear hug. Hugs always made my mom smile especially bear hugs full of love. Since that day, I have been trying to hug my mom every chance I get to show her how I feel.

From time to time to time, my mom and I read the Bible together. With her, I have read about many different virtues such as love, hope and faith. To me, all of them are important but love is the most important of all. What would life be like if there were no such thing as love? I think if there was no such thing of love, there would be no point of living.

I think there are plenty of ways people can use love. Every time you see somebody in need of love, cheer him or her up. If you listen to what I say and show love all the time, you will find there is a good feeling when you show love. You will feel proud of yourself knowing that you helped somebody, and you will want to show love all the time. That is a reason why I'll show love every day, all the time.

Chapter Six

Responsibility

RESPONSIBILITY

Keith M. Lattimore

Editors' Note: Keith Lattimore, a resident of Plainfield who describes his background at the start of this essay, served as a *Laws of Life* essay judge. He wrote this essay in the format of a letter intended to be read by the youth in Plainfield and similar locations.

My name is Keith M. Lattimore. I am a Police Captain, assigned as a Uniform Bureau Commander within the Plainfield, New Jersey, Police Division, completing my twenty-sixth year of service to the City of Plainfield. It is with great pride that I state that I am a product of the Plainfield Public School System, having graduated from Plainfield High School immediately prior to earning my B.A. degree (Sociology) from Rutgers College.

During my last two years of college and for four years thereafter, I substitute taught (mainly at the middle school and high school level) on a regular basis. I was also employed as program director of a youth center and as a youth counselor.

My experience as a substitute teacher and youth center leader, along with my later experience in law enforcement, has given me a chance to see students before and after they ran into serious difficulties. What became most obvious to me was that many of the former students who were disruptive, or acted in an irresponsible manner in school, were the same people who were paying frequent visits to our jail cells as adults. Individuals who were un-willing to follow school rules or respect the rights of others were often un-willing to follow the social rules or stay out of the way of the law later in life.

Having an arrest record as an adult, even for certain juvenile offenses can prevent a person from entering many fields of employment. Countless individuals who have been arrested in youth or in early adulthood have had to look back later in life with regret at their irresponsible behavior. It shattered some of their occupational plans, hopes and dreams.

On the other hand, many of those students who obeyed school rules, respected parental and school authority, showed regard for the rights of others and applied themselves diligently in their courses are now living happy and successful lives. They attained many of their personal and professional life goals. For these reasons, I consider responsibility to be one of my most essential Laws of Life. Some of the basic lessons which young people need to learn turn on this.

Lesson (1): Responsible and irresponsible behavior patterns are most often developed early in life. Deeply entrenched habits of acting irresponsibly are often very difficult to reverse. By contrast, well developed and long-term habits of responsible behavior make it easier to act correctly most of the time.

In just a few years, the generation of these student essayists will assume positions of power and leadership within the private and public sectors, inheriting the responsibility of determining the course of history. In light of the current, rapid and ever accelerating advances in technology, it seems reasonable to project the elimination of many jobs, and the rise of keen competition for those that are still available. Successful participation in the future job market will therefore require a strong educational background. Whether your ambition is to become a teacher, construction worker, police officer, chef, nurse, auto mechanic, research scientist, fashion designer, medical doctor or, yes . . . even a professional athlete (male or female), your ability to read, understand, access and apply information will be essential to your success. And, to do this well will require that you have a sense of responsibility.

I was blessed to be born to a great set of parents, both of whom were educators. Even though she was busy with raising seven children, my mother was able to supplement the household income through full-time teaching as we grew older.

My father was a pillar of the religious, educational, and political community. Throughout the entirety of my youth and young adulthood, he worked multiple jobs to help provide for our family- often more than sixteen hours per day. What was truly amazing was the fact that during the same period, he pursued post-graduate degrees on a part-time basis.

He developed and demonstrated a sense of responsibility in his early youth. From the age of eight, he would ride his bicycle from the 400 Block of West Fourth Street in Plainfield to Roselle, NJ (approximately eight miles one-way) after school and during summers to his grandfather's convenience store where he worked for years. Even though he later had a full athletic scholarship to college, he worked during both the summer (road repair and construction foreman) and the school year. He did this so that he could send money home to his mother to help support his seven brothers and sisters.

I, too, began work at a young age (10), doing odd jobs for neighbors, cutting grass, and shoveling snow. At eleven, I enjoyed the responsibility of managing my own daily newspaper route, which consisted of about seventy customers. Other early work experience ranged from being a store clerk to painting houses to working at a library desk, to being a road worker.

I always took the responsibilities of my jobs seriously and I still do, today. The Police Division Uniform Bureau consists of the Patrol Division, the Community Oriented Policing Unit, the Traffic Section, and Street Crimes unit. We employ 88 of the Division's 150 members. My current assignment makes me responsible for ensuring effective police service, public safety, and enforcement of law relative to the City of Plainfield. Further, I direct a number of other staff members, including police lieutenants, sergeants, police officers, and civilian personnel. From this, I draw another lesson about responsibility as a *Law of Life*:

Lesson (2): A strong work ethic, self-discipline, and responsible behavior serve to reinforce one another. Strive to attain and strengthen, or maintain and strengthen yourself in all three areas.

One of the things that my father told me in my youth about natural ability in the classroom or in athletics was "Son, it's not how much you have, but it's what you do with what you have." A generation later, one of the things that I said to our young daughter was ". . . it's not how much you have, but what you do with what you have. . .". From second grade onward, she would read, read, read— every book she could get her hands on. By the time she reached high school, not only had she continued her reading pattern, but she was also spending an average of four hours per night doing her homework and *studying*. Even with this commitment, she still dedicated numerous hours to practicing for and participating in the school color guard, along with other extracurricular activities.

Today, I am very proud to say that she has just completed her freshmen year at Harvard University, where she is an honors student and an editor of the school newspaper, and involved in numerous other extracurricular activities.

In retrospect, however, I cannot say that my advice alone impacted her development. She has always been a remarkably self-disciplined, self-motivated and responsible child/young adult. Further, my wife has been most instrumental in our daughter's educational success thus far. She has been a motivator, mentor, confidante, friend and so much more.

Not everyone has the same advantages that I did growing up. In some cases, one or both parents are absent. While some are reared by persons other than birth parent(s), who sometimes serve as far more effective and positive role models than the biological parent(s) do, others are less fortunate. And, some are from families whose financial situations place them at a significant disadvantage.

Life's journey does not always unfold for us along a straight or easy path. For most of us there will be obstacles along the way in the form of circumstances, events, and people that are sometimes beyond our immediate control.

However, disadvantage is no excuse to give up on school or life. A major source of satisfaction in attaining personal and occupational life goals is realizing that sometimes, it was sheer determination and willpower that made you able to overcome these obstacles. It probably also provided inspiration for others. Both presently and historically, many of those considered to be among the "greatest" within their field of endeavor have come from "disadvantaged" family backgrounds, including one former President of the United States. I have seen many people give in to disadvantage, but I have seen many others overcome it. From observing their heroic actions and remarkable great sense of responsibility, I can share another lesson about my *Law of Life*:

> *Lesson (3): Life is not fair. If it were, we would all be given an equal start. You can, however, level the playing field for yourself, for both your present and future family generations, for those whom you will be in a position to help, and those who choose to emulate you. Do this by always striving to be the very best person you can be, and by engaging in responsible behavior.*

Just imagine what a different world this would be if everyone did this – even if they did only the latter!

By way of conclusion, let me note that adults are responsible to provide love, be positive role models, impart proper social values, and give guidance and emotional support to the fullest extent possible. They thereby ensure that our young people can enter adulthood adequately equipped to be responsible, productive citizens, with the ability and motivation to utilize their full potential to achieve their life goals.

Whether or not the adults in your life have lived responsibly, you still need to be a responsible person. As a student or young adult, you are responsible to conform your behavior to the proper direction of your parents and teachers, obey school and civic authorities, and respect the rights of others. Further, it is most critical at this time in your life that you are as diligent in your schoolwork and studies as your energies permit. This leads to my final lesson, derived from responsibility as my *Law of Life*:

> Lesson (4): *Things just don't happen . . . they are made to happen. Be a responsible person. Make good things happen for you and those you care about most!*

MY BROTHER TAUGHT ME ABOUT RESPECT

Annastasia Johnson, 8th Grade

What is respect? What is responsibility? What do these ideas mean to you? To my brother, these ideas are his Laws of Life. He teaches them to me every day. To me, respect is treating someone the way you want to be treated. Responsibility is taking care of what needs to be done. I respect my elders, my family, especially my brother. My responsibilities involve doing well in school, and being a respectful accountable daughter and sister. My brother sets the pace.

I remember an argument I had with my mother. Teachers called my house and told her that I was misbehaving and talking too much with my friends. I thought my teachers were picking on me; that's what my friends always said. My mother yelled at me; I yelled back. That's when my brother stepped in. He calmed my mother down and said he would talk to me. "All your friends are trying to do is bring you down," he said. "You don't need that, you're smarter than that; you should be a leader, not a follower." He went on to say that he had many friends in school, but only a few had graduated with him. I began to understand his point.

When my brother was growing up, he didn't have any Laws of Life, and he didn't have anyone guiding him the way he guides me. He taught me the values of life, what to do, how to do it, when, where, and more. He teaches me everything I need to know to succeed. He always looks out for me and tells me the do's and don'ts, like "Don't talk in class," "Do all your work," and "Be your own person." I know these words may sound trite, but when he says them, I listen. I guess it's because he's so close to me in age that he still feels the sting of his own mistakes.

My brother teaches me respect like no one else. He always said to me, "Whenever you talk to somebody, look them straight in the eye so they know you're listening and being respectful." Every time I talk to somebody nowadays, I do this because I want him or her to know that I'm listening respectfully, that what he or she is saying is important.

My brother always stresses the importance of responsibility. As I watch him attend college, achieve good grades and maintain his part-time job, I wonder how he manages it all. A normal week for him goes like this: Monday, he works all day; Tuesday, he goes to classes all day; Wednesday he works, Thursday he attends classes; Friday, Saturday, and Sunday he works. That's responsibility; that's my brother. I know I'll be following in his footsteps when I attend college and have to manage my time. And, I know he'll be only a phone call away when things get demanding.

My brother has taught and is continuing to teach me many things. I admire him for his sense of respect and responsibility. Like he always says, "Everyone deserves respect, and you should always be responsible." He models my Laws of Life, for he follows them himself.

A SMALL DONATION

Nadira Foster-Williams, 5th Grade

A while ago I donated twenty dollars to the Masjid. By the way, a Masjid is a place where Muslims go to pray. I overheard my parents talking one day in the next room of our home. They were talking about the Masjid needing money for support. I thought about it for a moment and decided that I wanted to make a difference. Another reason I chose to do this was because I wanted to make my parents happy. I like to make them proud of me. They walked into the computer room. I said, "Not that I was in your business or anything, but I will donate fifty dollars to the Masjid," looking down at my feet.

My parents exchanged proud looks. (I was watching television mind you.) "Oh, may Allah (God) bless you," said my mom, "but twenty dollars will be fine."

I had a responsibility to help others whom were less fortunate. I was going out of my way to help many other people. "Are you sure you want to do this?" asked my dad. "I am sure," I said quickly, clutching the couch. My dad said something about Allah blessing me for giving, not being selfish, greedy and wanting more. I had made my decision, and I was proud if it. I was going to donate twenty dollars. I took some of my allowance and birthday savings and gave it to someone who needed it more than I did. I was so enamored with what I was about to do. I was taking money out of my account to give away to help someone else. I was saving my money to buy clothes for dolls, but this was much more important. This donation would change my life forever. I would live my life knowing I helped people who really needed it. I got the address of the Masjid from my parents and mailed my donation.

Months later, one Friday we went to Juman (Friday prayer service) and something shocking happened, something I never thought would happen. The Imam (religious leader) spoke about my donation! The Imam stated I would be recognized for my act of kindness at a luncheon and receive a certificate and lunch at one of the neighboring restaurants. That was one of the best days of my life. The *Laws of Life* that this experience represented for me were kindness, perseverance, and responsibility.

RESPONSIBILITY NEVER STOPS

Kimberly Villaneuva, 5th Grade

My mom is a responsible parent. Daddy and Mommy don't live together anymore, but mommy takes care of us by herself. It's not always easy for her. There have been times when there wasn't very much food. At one point, we even lived in a motel for four long months. Eventually, mom got a job cleaning up other people's houses. Even though she didn't like the work, she didn't stop. She was responsible for making sure we had a place to live and food to eat. Also, as soon as she found a house for us to live in, we moved out of the motel.

Our father didn't help mommy with money. Therefore, mommy had to find a better job. Now she works for the city of Plainfield, and her day is very busy because she works Monday through Saturday. Usually she gets very tired, but she doesn't stop working. She says, "One day we're going to be rich, and we won't have to worry about anything."

Nevertheless, when I grow up, I am going to get a good job that pays a lot of money, and when I have children of my own I can take good care of them. Mommy says, "Children are a blessing, and it's not a child's fault that their parents don't have very much money." She tells us that we are her children, and as long as she is living she will do her best to give us what we need.

My responsibility, for now, is to go to school everyday and always try to do my best. If there is something that I have to learn, that seems hard, I will keep on trying until I get it right. Therefore, when I am finished with school, I will get a good job. Like my mom, I will show up for work on time and do my best. I won't quit my job, even if it's hard. I will think of my mom and remember how hard it was for her to take care of three children by herself. I plan to save my money so that one day my children will have everything they need.

Furthermore, I believe that everyone can learn how to be responsible. No one is perfect. We all make mistakes, but if we understand that each day is a new one, we can correct our errors and try not to make the same mistakes twice. Life is good right now. All I have to do is go to school and learn. Our parents have given us a place to live in and food to eat. All of our needs are being met and my friends' lives are great too.

One day it will be my turn to make good choices and become fully responsible for myself and my family. I'm sure as I get older, I'll have more responsibility, but for now it's my turn just to enjoy being a kid.

RESPONSIBILITY CHANGES AS YOU GROW UP

Barell Williams, 5th Grade

Responsibility is taught at birth by your parents and by instincts. It is a baby's responsibility to let the parent know when it is hungry, tired or bored. The baby does this by crying. That is the very first form of responsibility you learn. As you grow up, your responsibilities change.

As a toddler, the only responsibilities I had was to remember never to talk to strangers, to look both ways when crossing the street and to respect my elders. As you grow up, responsibilities change. You either get more or less depending on how responsible and mature you are.

As a young adult I have a lot of responsibilities. There are a lot more things I have to remember to do and say. At home, I have to take out the garbage, clean my room and do my other chores. These are some examples of responsibilities. I also have to keep an eye on my little brother and sister while my mother is either cooking or taking a nap. If they were to get hurt, it would be my responsibility. It is also my responsibility to take care of the sneakers that cost my mother $100 to $200 dollars. If I don't, I will not get any more and that goes for everything that is bought for me.

At school, I have many responsibilities also. I have to turn in my homework, complete class assignments, and participate in class activities. If I do not, it will be my responsibility to explain to my mother why my grades are so terrible. For example if someone puts their hands on you in a hurtful manner it is your responsibility to tell a teacher. You are not supposed to hit them back; that is being irresponsible. A responsible person will follow all the rules.

On the street, your responsibilities are to say no to drugs, never drink or purchase alcohol. Cigarettes are bad for your health so do not let anyone pressure you into smoking. The responsible thing is to follow your heart. Remember to never take rides or talk to people you do not know. Last but not least, one of the most important responsibilities to remember is always strive to be and do your absolute very best.

OBLIGATIONS MAKE YOU RESPONSIBLE, BUT YOU DON'T HAVE TO LIKE THEM

Saquan Stevenson, 5th Grade

My essay is about responsibility, a definition of which is having obligations and being accountable. It also means being able to be trusted. Since I am the oldest of five children, I have many responsibilities. They include washing the dishes, taking out the garbage, cleaning the bathroom, and watching my brothers and sisters while my parents go out. At times, I do not like all of my responsibilities. It does not seem fair that I have all these jobs and my brothers and sisters don't. Other times, however, I feel proud that I have responsibilities because it means my parents trust me and put me in charge.

My responsibilities are not always bad. Sometimes they are good, like the times I get to go to the store. I get to go to Walgreens and buy food such as cereal, milk, and juice. I also enjoy going over homework with my brothers and sisters. It makes me feel proud that I can help them. I take my job of being responsible very seriously because if there was a fire I would have to get my brothers and sisters out safely.

I sometimes tell my Dad that I don't like my duties. He explains, "I give you jobs because it will teach you to be a responsible adult." From my responsibilities at home I have learned to be responsible in school. I do a great job by trying to get on the honor roll. I have my family and my wonderful teacher Miss Linnenman to thank. I try to encourage my brothers and sisters to do their best in school, so when they get to be my age they will be responsible.

We are all responsible for what happens on this planet. Littering in the oceans, cutting down trees, polluting the air, are some things we need to think about if we want to be responsible adults. This will help the next generation to know what their obligations to our planet will be.

SHOW RESPONSIBILITY EVERYWHERE

Elijah Smith, 5th Grade

The topic that I chose for my *Laws of Life* essay is responsibility. Responsibility means the state or fact of being responsible. As a student, being responsible means making sure you have your class assignments completed, your homework is done, eating properly, and going to bed early. We must always do our best.

There are many ways to show responsibility. My responsibilities at home are to take out the garbage, recycling, vacuum the carpet, clean the bathroom and clean my bedroom. My parents always tell me that I do a fine job too.

When showing responsibility you may be recognized by your teacher, parents, friends, family and even your principal. Also, you can get a job and earn money, or a scholarship for school. Sometimes when you show responsibility you can receive lots of rewards. For example, if you want your mom to buy you a dog, you ask for it but your mother and father say, "We have to wait and see what your report card looks like. If we see you've done well, then you can have the dog." We are always supposed to show responsibility wherever we go because the younger kids are watching us. You see, as pre-teens, we are supposed to set a good example while we are at school and everywhere else. If we fight or curse, that isn't showing responsibility. We must learn to be polite to one another.

In conclusion, the lesson I learned from this essay is we are always supposed to show responsibility everywhere we go. Do you know why? Because someone may be watching us. Furthermore we should have enough respect for our self to respect others. By being responsible, remember you can earn your degree and a scholarship. It can have a great effect on your life and maybe someone else's too.

STAYING STRONG FOR MY FAMILY

Keyonnah Williams, 5th Grade

I have one law of life. It is responsibility. I have a lot of responsibilities in my life. I am the oldest of my three little sisters and we all are in a very bad situation.

When my mom was incarcerated the first time for two years, I was living with my grandmother. My grandmother was very sick. She had diabetes. She was in and out of the hospital and she was very worried about my mom. That put more pressure on her.

When my mom came home it seemed like everything was going right until that one day my uncle came to my house early in the morning and said, "Your mother is calling for you." They took us to our cousin's house and they went to the hospital. When they got there it was too late. My grandmother was deceased. My mom told me that night it felt like the whole world had ended for her.

I knew I had to stay strong for my mom and my little sisters. That was my biggest responsibility. My mom got into some more trouble and this caused her to get incarcerated the second time. However, before her second incarceration, she was phoning people, and she was trying to find someone to take care of us before she had to go away again. She said we were going to a family of strangers. I was very worried because I saw my mom get arrested and I knew my grandmother was no longer there. I wondered where we would go.

Thank God, she had a friend whose mother was so kind as to take us in. I did not even know her and she did not know us. She had us for seven months now but it seems like seven years because we are so close. She treats us like one of her own.

When my mom got out, she got messed up again and she does not know what she wants in life. I know what I want in life. I see what my life is about: responsibilities! That is my law of life.

Chapter Seven

Family/Relationships

THE IMPORTANCE OF FAMILY
RELATIONSHIPS IN OUR LIVES

Albert McWilliams

Editors' Note: Albert McWilliams was the Mayor of Plainfield at the time he wrote this essay; his son Albert wrote an essay on Love. Shortly before the publication of this book, we learned of the untimely death of Mr. McWilliams due to illness. We know this essay expresses some of his deepest feelings about his own family, which will always feel the void of his passing while also always cherishing the loving inspiration of their memories of him.

A comforting smile or touch or hug at unsettling moments, quiet encouragement when things seemingly are not going well, laughter at a joke nobody outside the family even gets, wrestling and pillow fights, being lovingly nursed back to health, help with homework, fishing, bicycling, getting dressed up to go to church or to a wedding or to a funeral or some other special occasion, sitting there crying or cringing in fear or cracking up at a movie, crying at a birth or a death or a major disappointment, tenseness while hoping that a loved one succeeds in a competition, singing "Happy Birthday," listening to certain Christmas songs for the umpteenth time, learning the latest slang or dance moves…oh, how I could go on. These are just some of the memories that immediately come to my mind when I think about family relationships. And it is these powerful experiences that make family relationships one of my *Laws of Life*.

Of all of the blessings God has bestowed upon me, my relationships with my mother, my father, my sisters and other family as I was growing up down in Atlanta, and with my wife and her family and our five children today, are at the top of the list.

Everyone's family is unique. Like games of chess, no two ever go exactly the same way. Yet, every family relationship is important, too. Family relationships can make you strong, they can break you down (sometimes for the better), they can make you prosper or make you go broke, but they always leave their mark on your life. To paraphrase the Bible's book of Proverbs, we sharpen each other by relating to each other, as iron sharpens iron.

We live in an age where just about everything is studied. And, with the advent of the internet, the data from those studies are readily accessible to everyone. Family relationships are no exception. The "experts" have written volumes about the importance of family. While their conclusions might seem like good old common sense to many of us, I believe many of their findings worth repeating.

Here is a fascinating conclusion from several academic studies. All things being equal, children from strong families consistently do better in every measure of well-being than their peers who do not have strong family relationships. Strong family relationships are more important to a person's success in life than race, family economic status and even educational attainment. Imagine that! A strong family can overcome the evils of racism, poverty and even a lack of education. Now that is powerful.

Communities with a greater number of strong families tend to be safer and better places to live, and are less likely to have substance abuse and crime among their young people. Why? Because strong families are more likely to provide the security and supervision their children need and thus to discourage them from substance abuse and crime. Strong families also reduce the financial and social costs of drug abuse and crime, and they enable more young people to finish school and grow up to be productive, intelligent adults.

The positive impact of strong family relationships goes way beyond their impact on us as individuals. It extends to society in general. I see this everyday, especially in my role as Mayor of Plainfield, New Jersey. One of the reasons I wanted to become Mayor is to create a community with such strong families, as a way to live out my *Law of Life*. People with strong family relationships are more likely to engage in civic activities, such as voting and community work. The hundreds of families who participate in our community help our city to remain vibrant and resourceful. Parents are almost twice as likely as those without children to volunteer in social service projects. They tend to know more about their neighbors, and are more likely to participate in civic and school organizations and to take their children to church. People from strong families also have lower rates of depression and anxiety, better physical health, and longer life-spans. And, they engage less in excessive drinking, drinking and driving, and drug use and smoking, because they have a sense of meaning, obligation, and constraint. Children from such families also enjoy better physical health and have fewer emotional and behavioral problems. There are also fewer suicides among this group. Healthier people are less likely to be absent from their jobs; they also miss fewer days of school. Strong families create more vital communities, in which people look after one another and take seriously their responsibilities as citizens.

A story about award-winning author Patricia McKissack has always made a big impression on me and has influenced my Laws of Life. Evidently, when she was growing up, she listened to her grandfather tell stories of how he and his brother left Nashville when they were seventeen and eighteen and headed north to Chicago in search of opportunity. Years later, when she recalled her grandfather mentioning that they arrived in Chicago at the time of some terrible riots, she realized that her grandfather and his brother had been in the city during the Chicago Riot of 1919. Ms. McKissack says, "When asked how he survived those trying times, my grandfather used one word: 'Family'."

Except for faith in God, my experiences tell me that, beyond a shadow of a doubt, that there is no Law of Life that is more important in life than strong, positive family relationships. If each one of us, young or old, took this to heart, our communities would be better places for us all. Regardless of our race or economic status, strong family relationships can enable us to achieve what we desire. It all begins at home.

MY LIFE INSPIRATION

William Morris, 8th Grade

"My grandmother has taught me many things including the family values and love of life."

It was an exciting Christmas morning, 2001. I could not wait to open my gifts from my grandmother. I was not really expecting a lot of things from her this year, but I was sure she would surprise me. Even though my grandmother was short on money that Christmas, she still managed to buy me a sixty dollar Kwanzaa Ball ticket, pajama pants, and an expensive outfit. From Christmas through the rest of the week, my spirits were high. My grandmother has four grandchildren and I am the only boy. Out of all the love she has to give to the other three, she manages to save just enough love to make me feel like the only one she has.

My grandmother has always been the one to put things back together when they have gone off track. Whenever something went wrong with my mom and me, she would always extend her hand to me. She has taught me the value of the world family, and has shown me that one person's love and kindness can go a very long way. For some reason, my grandmother always had a happy spirit no matter what happened during the day, good or bad. When my mind is mixed up from some bad situation, her presence has always cheered me up.

For as long as I can remember (from about six years of age) I have been going to the Shiloh Baptist Church with my grandmother. After I turned nine, I joined the choir. It is named God's Gift of Praise. To this day, I am still with them.

My grandmother taught me that it was important to attend as many family gatherings and reunions as possible. She said something I will never forget: "Never let anything stop you from being with your family, because tomorrow is not promised to anyone." There is plenty more to tell, but it would take more than a lifetime to write all of it down.

The last family reunion I attended was on Labor Day Weekend 2006. It was an eight hour drive to Rocky Mount, North Carolina with my aunt. I had to ride with her because my mom could not go for some reason. My grandma made arrangements for me to ride down there with her sister, Ernestine, because there was no more room left in her car. Being the person she is, she made sure I would get there. I think she did it because she knew I had planned for a long time to go. That is what you call a compromise made out of love.

All things considered, my *Law of Life* is to always have a mind filled with love and to inspire someone besides myself. Surely, my grandma has given to me all the good that was inside her. When I think of her, I think of an Angel sent from God. When it comes down to all the nitty-gritty, I always think of her happy state of mind. That way, I can keep my head up and show people that there are good things in this world. In order to improve my character, I will begin to be a leader and especially a role model for my younger peers. I want people to see my positive attitude one day, too. Someone may be inspired by me in the same way that I was inspired by my grandmother.

MY FATHER'S LIFE SHOWS ME
WHAT IT MEANS TO BE SUCCESSFUL

Vanessa Jimenez, 8th Grade

My father is a real important person to me. He is one person who has provided many of the laws of my life. He helps me think about the consequences of making the right choices on a good path and those of making the wrong choices on a bad path. My father doesn't obligate me to do anything, but he explains to me what the consequences of making important decisions might be.

Not only does he help me and other members of his family, but he has helped people that he doesn't even know. For example, two days before Christmas one year, he went to a foreign country and bought groceries for ten different homes. In that country, people have very little food and almost no money. These people were so grateful that they began to cry when they saw they could feed their children a full dinner on Christmas.

My father has inspired a lot of people to be successful in life. Many couples have come to him to be the god-father of their weddings or of their children. When friends or relatives need advice or other help, they come to him. They feel the same way I feel about him.

He has done many things in his life that have shown me the many laws of life. I remember once he was driving through a run-down area and a very old man and women went up his window and asked him to give them a coin. He gave them a bill instead. They were so happy that they thanked him many times.

Money isn't a law of life. Sometimes being honest to yourself makes you feel good and causes you to become a better person. Definitely my father hasn't always been at the top. He knows what it is to be poor. I believe when people haven't had things for their whole life, they appreciate them more. He is also a very hard-working man. He has earned all he has with his bare hands and by the sweat of his brow. You can't properly follow the *Laws of Life* when you earn easy and dirty money. He's a businessman who knows how to do his things. He's taught me a lot of things about how to become a successful hard working businesswomen when I grow up. I really appreciate having him in my life and teaching me all that I know.

He has shown me that respect too is a very important quality, and that it helps you get through life. He teaches us that in respecting others, we respect ourselves, and that we cannot believe we are better than anyone else. Treating everyone the same is important to him. No matter what race, religion, or age they are, everyone deserves respect.

My father is my role-model and the mirror for my own success. He has shown me all the *Laws of Life* because he has lived them.

MY MOM SHAPES MY LIFE

Veronica Garcia, 8th Grade

The person who has helped me to shape my life is the one person whom I love most in the world, my mom. She is caring, honest, trustworthy, loyal, respectful, loving, and the list goes on and on. I respect her for who she is and she won't change for anyone. She is a role-model and a perfect example of a hardworking and loving mother. I am proud to say that I love her and consider her one of my best friends.

One of the things that she has taught me is to always speak my mind. My mom will always give her honest opinion on everything, even though the truth may sometimes hurt. Another thing that I admire about her is how hard she works. She is a single mother raising my sister, my two brothers and me. She always wants us to have the best, no matter what.

My mom has also taught me a lot. Even though she may not know it, I look up to her because she is such a strong woman. She has always set a positive example for me and the rest of our family. The one thing that I love most about her is the advice that she gives us and the stories she tells us about her life. They always have a meaning or a moral that she hopes we will learn.

My mom is truly the one person who has most shaped my life.

THE PERSON I ADMIRE MOST

Antwan McLean, 5th Grade

The person I admire most in my life is my grandmother. I admire her because she taught me a lot of things that will make me a good person.

She said that if someone gives you something to always say thank you. But the most important thing she taught me was to respect others: "Always give your teachers and friends respect," she would say. "They will respect you back even more!"

My grandmother is also the only person who helped me solve my problems. She would make sure that everything was all right. If I needed some money for the book fair, she always gave it to me. We did a lot of activities together, too, like putting up the Christmas tree, playing games, going to the movies and especially cooking. Cooking was what we most liked doing. Every weekend we would cook. She taught me how to cook macaroni and cheese, mashed potatoes, homemade gravy and fried chicken. She also taught me how to play cards. She always talked to me about doing well in school and about the danger of drugs and hanging out on the streets. She made me promise to care for my little brother and sister when she passes away.

I loved my grandmother and she loved me. She was more like my real mother because she took care of me and made sure that I had clean clothes, food and was happy. When my grandmother became sick I helped my aunt take care of her. I helped to take care of her because she had always taken care of me. It was my turn to help. I took my grandmother to the park in her wheelchair for some fresh air. When her eyes became bad I would put the insulin into her needle so that she could give herself a shot. I also prepared the pills she was going to take.

I was very sad when she died. I felt very alone. No one will ever fill the place in my heart that I have for her. I know that I will grow up to be a better person because of having my grandmother in my life. I will never forget her and will forever remember the things she taught me about respect, pride and always doing my best.

ABUELITO AND MY ADMIRATION FOR HIM

Charles Riascos, 5th Grade

The person I admire is 6 feel tall and a lot older than me. He has gray hair, caramel colored skin, and brown eyes. He has been there for me when I had problems or just as a friend. He is my Abuelito in Colombia.

"Do the right things Charles. Choose those things that will help you in life. Always be smart." My grandfather always helped me out when I needed him. One time, my Father cooked meat with onions. I was disgusted at the thought of eating the onions. "Abuelito will you eat my onions?"

"Yes Charles. Just give them to me."

Everyday after school, my sister Angie and I would come home. I'd open the door and see my grandfather sitting on the rocking chair just waiting for me.

"Buenas Tardes Abuelito. How was your day?"

"Fine, how was your day in school?"

"It was great. Hey Abuelito, when I finish my homework I can help you with anything you need?" I liked helping my Grandfather. It was very fun because we would have the chance to sit and talk together. He was different from my parents and other adults. He kept secrets and listened to all my stories.

The last time I saw Abuelito was not such a fun time. We were at my Abuelita's home in Buenaventura, Colombia. It was a rainy morning at 4:00 a.m. I was feeling sleepy but concerned about what I would do the next day without my friends. That next day was the day I would leave Colombia and go to America with my Papi and Angie.

My sister, Papi and I formed a line so we each had our chance to say good-bye to Tia Nora, Tio Jackson, Abuelita, and Abuelito. Angie was first and was sure to give everyone a hug. But my Abuelito not only received a hug but the sign of the cross to show she would remember him.

When it was my turn I went directly to my grandfather. I gave him strong hug that let him know I cared about him. Then I raised my index finger to my forehead, then to my chest, next to my left shoulder, then to the right one, and last to my lips. The sign was sure to let him know I would never forget him.

My sister and I moved to the porch and my Father stayed inside hugging my grandfather while he cried. It made me cry also seeing my strong father appear so small and hurt. Our next destination was Cali and then America.

I remember so many things about Abuelito like how he had so many hats, and that he has the same face as me only older. But, what I remember always is how he loved me and wanted the best for me in America. I found admiration in a person who is 6 feel tall and a lot older than me.

A NEW KIND OF FAMILY

Jasmine Jimenez, 5th Grade

Just the four of us, my Mom, my Dad, my brother and me lived together as a family. My Mom and Dad argued a lot, but now that they are not together they are both happy. I am happy also, because I didn't like the fights, but sometimes I wished that they would get back together. Now, I visit my Dad in Florida during the summer and I live with my Mom and brother during the school year. I miss my Mom when I am in Florida. When I am in New Jersey with my Mom, I miss my Dad.

My mom recently remarried and my Dad now has another family which includes a daughter who is one year old. I also have a new stepsister and stepbrother, they are my stepfather's children. My stepsister is 14 and my stepbrother is 15. They live with their mother but every other weekend they come to visit their father and stay at our house. I am really excited about going to Florida this summer because I will get to see my little sister for the first time. I use to think that there was only one kind of family, a mother, father and their kids. Now I know that there can be more than one kind of family. Who said that family is just a mother, father and children? Family is people who love each other and that's more important than whether or not we fit someone else's image. I like when my step-brother and sister come over to my house. They don't talk to me that much but I think it's because we don't really know each other yet. When we get to know each other we will begin to feel more like a family.

Chapter Eight

Self-Discipline

SELF-DISCIPLINE AND THE GOLDEN RULE

Cheryl Nagel-Smiley

Editors' Note: Cheryl Nagel-Smiley introduced *Laws of Life* to her 8th grade students in Special Education classes at Hubbard Middle School in Plainfield. From that moment, she has used them in ways that her students and colleagues have found especially inspiring. One of her students was among the first group of winners of the 8th grade *Laws of Life* Essay Contest in Plainfield.

Discipline has many interpretations. To a child, discipline can mean a "time out," sitting in the corner, removal of a favorite toy or activity, and perhaps, even a spanking. To the student, discipline comes in classroom rules, school rules, "The Golden Rule," and even the rules of peer relationships. The law and the police are the disciplinarians for adults, while military personnel follow unconditional orders no matter the price.

The most important type of discipline is "self discipline"—and the key to this is the word "self." Discipline, no matter how lenient or strict, only comes into play when the main focus is on "self" control. As a teacher of special need students for almost four decades, I have seen the state and federal laws change to accommodate that population of students. In the past, they were educated by being shut off in dark, dingy, subterranean classrooms. But, presently, they enjoy full mainstreaming and in-class support. Still, even though the laws have changed over the last fifty years, students' advancement clearly depends on their own "self" discipline. In other words, if they possess self discipline, they will learn in spite of their surroundings.

Children should be taught the art of self-discipline from a very early age. Their parents and other important role models can impose this upon them. Discipline cannot first be taught at age five when children enter kindergarten. By that point, it should already be deeply embedded in a child's demeanor.

How does a young toddler learn discipline? A young child learns from the examples and modeling of those who love him or her. It is beneficial to discipline a child and there are many ways to do it. Children should be involved in activities that require practice, team work, and motivation. These help develop sound routines and lead to a sense of satisfaction in achievement.

My mother tells the story of how, at age three, I "stole" a can of tuna fish while grocery shopping with her. She took me by the hand and led me back into the store, where, holding the tuna fish, I was confronted by the store manager and had to repeat to him the deeds of my "crime." Coincidentally, at a similar age, my son stole a pack of gum. Unlike in my case, where I couldn't open the can of tuna, he managed to chew a stick of the gum. But, I also took him back into the store, holding the rest of the gum and fifty cents from his piggybank. He also was confronted by the store manager, admitted his "crime" and paid for his mistake.

Students in my classroom know that "honesty is always the best policy." No matter how angry or upset I may become, it is quickly forgotten when resolved. They also know that a lack of trust is a dark shadow forever encircling the class. I model self-discipline for them and never utter the wrong message such as "Do as I say, not as I do." I have not missed a class for over fifteen years, take good care of my appearance, and, above all, take and show pride in my work.

As a single mother, I knew it wasn't going to be easy raising a son. I involved him in all the introductory sports—t-ball, baseball, soccer, basketball, gymnastics, and swimming. At age six, he fell in love with swimming and participated in both summer and winter swim teams. Discipline fell right into place. He knew homework had to be completed, dinner eaten, and everything readied for the next day before going to practice. Swim meets were important because you couldn't let down the team. The self-discipline involved in those early years has definitely paid off. As a high school student, he was very involved in all activities—swimming, track, cross country, student council, National Honor Society and other clubs. He held elected office positions in many of them. Now as a college student his self-discipline has gotten him over those difficult times that most college students face.

In a world where many lack self-discipline, tolerance of others, and openness to new ideas, schools should emphasize the three R's—responsibility, respect, and resilience- and an "S"—for self-discipline. It is only when we start to discipline our own lives and free ourselves of our own absurd behaviors, inspire motivation, acknowledge and enhance moral–values and live "The Golden Rule" that we will start to see overall improvements in our schools and in our lives.

TAKING CARE OF ME

Rachel Barnes, 11th Grade

During the last two years of high school, most students like myself, are trying to prepare for college or any other post-secondary education. In order to be successful in college, you need to stay focused in high school and develop your laws of life. My primary law of life is to keep my priorities in line. My priorities are my well-being, education, and future.

First of all, I believe that my well-being is very important. This includes my physical, emotional, and spiritual health. If I don't take care of myself in these areas, I won't be able to function properly. My goal is to become a highly effective person so that I can be successful in life. To achieve this, I will take steps now so that I can apply it to every aspect of my life in the future.

I already know that things like alcohol and drugs will destroy my body, therefore, I will not be tempted to consume these substances now or in the future. I know that these things will only weaken my physical health. I need to develop healthy eating habits and maybe do some exercise. I will also monitor my health under the supervision of a physician I can trust. Managing my time better will keep me from becoming stressed, which can wear you out and make you tired. Practicing these habits will improve my health and produce satisfying results.

Emotional and spiritual health is the key to having a strong sense of who I am. I have a positive self-image and self-esteem. However, at times I do doubt myself. This is natural though, because I am still growing up and I know that no one is perfect. The best way to maintain emotional health for me is to stay positive and focus on my future. Spiritual health is having peace, and for me that means having faith in God to guide and direct me. Praying and reading the Bible brings me closer to God and gives me insight to the true meaning of life. If my spiritual health is in shape, then I will remain emotionally stable.

Education is another one of my priorities. I have my mind set on becoming a pediatrician. To be any type of doctor takes years of devotion and time. You need the proper education to earn a degree and practice in this field.

Therefore, I will not hesitate to make the best of my education. I feel that education is a great opportunity and I will receive the full benefits of it by working hard.

If I take care of my well-being and get my education, I am bound to have a successful future. With these things in mind, I feel I will do well in college. I also need to learn responsibility, and respect others and myself. While I am in college, I will be able to take the initiative to get things done as an adult would. I will be able to enjoy new experiences and handle any difficult situations that a college student is faced with.

Since I come from a predominately black town and school system, I will go to a diverse college. Surrounding myself with people of many different types will help me gain a better understanding of different cultures. It will also prepare me for when I go into the workplace. I will be able to work with various people more easily. In conclusion, if I begin to develop my *Laws of Life* now, I will be very successful as a college student and working adult.

SELF-CONTROL IS INNER STRENGTH

Devin Austin, 5th Grade

I can't tell you when I kept my self-control, but I can tell you when I lost it and I regained it. It was about two years ago. My grandpa was very sick. I feared that he was sick enough to pass away.

That night my grandma told me that my grandpa was at the hospital. I had a dream that night about him there. The next day my mom called me into her room with a sad sounding voice. She told me that my grandpa had been pronounced dead the day before. I felt a tear roll down my cheek. I couldn't believe that my role model passed away. I didn't even get a chance to say good-bye.

For the next few days I didn't keep my self-control. I was angry with any one that spoke to me. I was afraid that I would hurt someone if they annoyed me. When I went home, my mom called me into her room again. I was hoping that she wasn't going to give me any bad news. She asked me what was wrong. I said, "It's just that when my grandpa passed away I felt like I lost a part of me." "Me too" she replied. The next day I was on my way to my room when my brother bumped into me and I did something that I regret until this day. I punched him in the stomach. I apologized as much as I could. That night I had a dream that my grandpa was still alive. He was in pain from his condition. When I woke from my dream, I understood that he died so he wouldn't be in any more pain. The day of the funeral, I admit that I cried but only with my mom. At that time I felt closer to her than ever before. I tried to keep my self-control the whole time. I learned a lesson. If you don't want to do something that you will regret later, think first and have self control. It helps to see the grown up side of things.

SELF-DISCIPLINE IS MY LAW OF LIFE

Jamari Miller, 5th Grade

Do you have self-discipline? Well, I remember when I was in the second grade and my teacher used to stress me out yelling at me. One day, I realized that I had no self-discipline because I threw a chair at her. At that moment, I knew there would be consequences. I hadn't thought before I acted.

The teacher called my Mom, and she arrived at the school furious. I knew she was mad at me from the time she came in the door. She didn't say one word to me. Next, I got into her car and, to my surprise, we were at the Plainfield Police Station. It didn't take long either. That's when she said these nine words. "This is where people go with no self-discipline."

That is when I met Officer Christmas. He gave me the lecture of my life. He scared me for about one hour by putting me in the juvenile jail, telling me to throw the bench that was nailed to the wall. I cried, and told him I couldn't. He yelled at me in a deep voice, "Stay there while I talk to your mother." It seemed like they talked forever. My mom told him all the things I had been doing wrong. Then he told her that he would handle it today. Officer Christmas took me on a tour of the jail. Later, he sat me down and told me about negative and positive behaviors. Plus he told me about all of the kids that he sees at that jail with no self-discipline. He gave me things that I could do to keep my temper calm, for example, count to ten, talk to a friend or talk to my mom. He said, "No one will be by your side like she will."

Today, I've learned to control my temper. I sometimes struggle, but I often remember two things: I don't want to go to jail, now or ever. And, my grandmother taught me something important, too, the fear of GOD. So, I think about what I've been through, and I try to stay calm.

Now that I'm in the fifth grade, I believe self-discipline is important and I will continue to use this law of life throughout my journey here. I believe success is the best. I will further my education after high school by going to Morehouse College to become an architect. I am using this law of life, "Self-Discipline!"

SELF-CONTROL OVER MY MIND AND BODY

Denzel Seals, 5th Grade

The *Laws of Life* include self-discipline, respect, responsibility, perseverance, honesty, fairness, and kindness. The law of life that I use is self-discipline.

Self-discipline is self-control and training of oneself. What it means in my words is to have control over my mind and body. For example, one day I was angry because my third grade teacher gave me a score below a 100. I started to get rambunctious. Then I thought about the consequences that lay ahead. I decided to have self-control and the perseverance to try again and to do better. From that day on, I tried to always work harder and be self-disciplined.

Many people in this world need self-discipline. Self-discipline affects the community. The incidence of crimes decreases when people practice self-control. With self-discipline more families would live in a peaceful society and enjoy a good quality of life. When that happens, it will make our community safe and encourage new people to move in. Overall, our social lives will improve.

A place where self-discipline should definitely be practiced is in school, when students are developing their talents. If they do not have any self-discipline, they will not develop good study habits, or a sense of respect for authority and parents. When these young people become adults, they will not have quality citizenship skills to transfer to their children.

In America, there is a lot of school violence because students do not use self-discipline. Most of America's youth engage in fights, drugs, and shootings, especially at the high schools. On April 20, 1999, 14 students and one teacher got killed at Columbine High School in Littleton, Colorado. On May 1999, six students were wounded at Heritage High School in Conyers, Georgia. On January 10, 2001, a 17-year old was killed by a police officer after he fired shots and took hostages at a high school north of Los Angeles. These are only a few examples. Several violent acts occur everyday.

I know many people are hurt because of school violence. Although I do not know how it feels to lose a loved one, I think that whoever starts school violence should also feel the pain that the victims' families and friends have felt. If people who committed crimes had self-discipline, these heart-breaking incidents would not happen.

If I can start a program or a club to support kids to develop good social skills, I will. Through the activities that will run at the program site, the kids will do better at school and at home.

Without self-discipline the world would be a difficult place to live because there would be no respect. Kids would have no education and they would be violent. There would be no love, honesty, courage, kindness, fairness, respect, and perseverance. Without all of those laws of life, this world would be an impossible place.

I want to encourage young people to take the *Laws of Life* as their guide. It will help them in this life. It will make today better and turn them into better citizens tomorrow.

CAN YOU KEEP YOUR SELF-ESTEEM?

Eveanandi Butler, 5th Grade

It was the first day of second grade. I was going to a new school called Abington Elementary in Newark, NJ. Fall had come and everything was bright, beautiful, and colorful. The atmosphere put me in a good mood. Nothing was going to ruin my day. I remember my Mom and Dad telling me to be careful. They told me to stay away from certain people who were rude and nasty. I didn't take this warning seriously. I was not going to let anything ruin my day.

When I got to school, I realized what my parents were talking about. Most of the people were nice, I noticed two boys. They were the people my parents were talking about. This is where my law of life comes in. My law of life is self-esteem and I needed a lot of it then. These boys liked to torment people and I was their number one target. They made fun of me because of my last name (which is Butler). The boys liked to tease me because I am African-American and Indian. But the one thing that they would tease me about the most was the fact that I was smarter than many students. They called me very rude names whenever they got a chance. I didn't let this bother me. I ignored what they said.

Soon I talked to my parents about what happened. They told me that keeping my self-esteem and not letting the boys bother me was a very good way of handling my situation. My parents told me that this would help me stay on track in life. They told me that if I knew that I was important, I would be able to over come any problem in life.

So, I kept my self-esteem. I stayed away from the boys. When they called me names, I remembered what my parents told me. I wasn't going to let them hurt me. Soon the two bullies realized that their name-calling and teasing wasn't bothering me anymore and they stopped.

When I understood that keeping my self-esteem helped me, I started to teach my sisters the same thing. I told them that it was something that you have for yourself. It is when you believe in yourself and you don't let anyone get you down. I told them that it is important for everyone to have high self-esteem.

Now that I am in fifth grade and I look back on what happened in second grade, I realize that the bullies were so unimportant. I can't remember their names. This is funny because they tried so hard to make me feel bad. I still believe in self-esteem and it helps me a lot when someone tries to put me down.

I kept my self-esteem even though it was very hard. Can you keep yours?

SELF-DISCIPLINE AND SELF-DETERMINATION

Anonymous, 5th Grade

Have you ever had to use self-determination and self-discipline for any thing in your life you had a problem with? If you haven't, one day you will. That's why my essay is about these things.

I was five years old when I had this experience. I was going to my first gymnastics class in the summer of 1995. I was a little scared because I did not know what would happen, and I was nervous because it was my first time and I was afraid of not having friends. I had a small diary. So, on our way there in the car, I wrote down all my feelings about what was going to happen. The gymnastics class was in Edison, New Jersey where my aunt lives. My little cousin, Tonelle, lives there, too. My cousin was going to gymnastics with me, and so was my sister Destiny. When I realized that, I was not so scared. I was thinking that I might be in the same group with them and kind of felt better. But what I forgot was that I am two years older than both of them. So, when I got there, I was not with them after all. I was in one with older kids, one that required more advanced work. My Mom dropped off the others and then walked me to my class. When I got there, my teacher was at the door, so she and my Mom met. They shook hands and I was introduced to the teacher. I said hello to be polite even though I was shy and nervous. My knees were shaking and I had butterflies in my stomach. Then I looked inside my class-room and saw so many kids that were so tall (well at least taller than me!). I was even more nervous than before, and was thinking, "Oh my gosh, what if they pick on me?" And, "What if I don't like it here?" or "I'm nervous," "I don't want to go," "I'm scared." But then I swallowed my pride, found some courage and slowly walked inside the classroom with my eyes half shut. The teacher told us to sit in a circle and we did. I was sitting next to a tall skinny girl, but I did not know her name, and a heavyset boy with curly hair. He was average height. The teacher told us what we were going to learn–cartwheels. Everyone was excited except me because I was scared that they might laugh at me. I did not know how to do one, and, in my head, I was thinking, "What if I fall down, and they laugh and I get embarrassed?" But then my self-determination kicked in. In the back of my mind, I was thinking, "I can do this!" "I'm determined to learn this flip, I want to learn it and I'm going to try my best to do this cartwheel." So I stood up in the row and got enough space around me and was waiting for the instructor to teach us.

"Okay class, now place your left foot in front of you and both hands out in front of you," she told us.

"Now, place your hands on the ground and flip your body over to the other side." She directed us. Everyone did the steps as directed, and flipped their body over. I did the flip and fell on the ground. I did not make it. I felt mad and sad. Then I had noticed that the heavyset boy did not make it either but kept trying again and again until he got it right. Then the teacher came over and said, "You will get the flip sooner or later, and right now I will help you get through it." Then I heard laughing. They were laughing at me. I was angry. I wanted to hit someone but I couldn't. That is when my self-discipline came in. I had to control myself not to hit anyone or I would get laughed at and teased more. I would get into in big trouble, and still not be able to do a cartwheel. But for the next couple of days, I used my two new *Laws of Life* skills and it really helped me get through those days. And, everyday I practiced and practiced.

It was two months later. I had practiced everyday and used self-discipline and self-determination also during that time. Then the first day of the next month, the instructor told us "Okay now, you all know it's been two months, and I want to see how much you all improved in your cartwheels. I will call you one by one to show me." Eventually, it was my turn. I got up and held my head high, and felt a warm tingle in my body. I then looked over at my teacher, she smiled at me and I was determined to do this flip. I took the steps, step by step, and then all that hard work paid off, because now I could do a cartwheel. I was happy. My teacher came over and patted me on my back and she said, "I knew you could do it, I'm proud of you!" And she gave me a big smile. So I smiled at her. I felt happier than ever, I was glad to have accomplished something and, in the middle of it all, saw that I had used two new *Laws of Life* skills to do it.

This helps me look forward to future activities, for instance, cheerleading. I can do flips for that. I feel happy and proud of myself. I can look back and know I achieved something on my own at a young age. I also realized that I can be my best I by using the skills to accomplish something that was complicated and difficult for me at the time. And, I know that I did things right. These are my *Laws of Life*!

Chapter Nine

Honesty

HONESTY

Gloria F. Royster

What an exciting experience I had as a reader for the *Laws of Life* initiative! The young people who submitted essays proved that they are well aware of the values that the *Laws of Life* attempt to impart. It is a double pleasure to introduce the chapter on "Honesty" because this value encompasses all the characteristics of the others.

Honesty is the best policy—a phrase which is trite but true. The statement is one that should be enshrined at the start of every activity. Honesty means there are no contradictions or discrepancies in thoughts, words or actions. Being honest with oneself engenders trust from both self and others and it inspires faith as well. This is where our work as adult mentors begins. We must set examples which earn trust and inspire faith.

Being honest also means telling the truth even when it hurts. This is one quality that both small children and older people have in common: They are brutally honest. Has a youngster ever told you that your teeth are crooked? Or has an old person called you stupid? I find myself nearest to the latter group, since I find it increasingly less difficult to speak my mind with impunity. There comes a time in life when you must stop stressing over what you say and how you express yourself and simply be honest.

As a young mother, I found it very difficult to turn down salesmen on the phone and would allow him/her to make a pitch. Even though I dreaded talking with them, I still could not allow my sons to tell them that I wasn't home, because I realized that even though the person on the phone would not be aware of my status, my children knew. Had I allowed my children to simply reply, "She's not home," I would have been sending the wrong message to them. I could not do that but instead had to set boundaries. This does not imply that children will be honest as a result, but it does play a powerful role in their development as honest human beings. I am old enough now to simply tell the caller that I am not interested and hang up. (Senior privilege!)

When boundaries are set at home, they are carried into the community. Children will not get sticky fingers and bring home strange toys and games that you did not buy. They also will not bring home fabricated stories for you to sort out. Very young children are naturally honest, but they lose that when we impart the message that some forms of dishonesty are okay. Ambiguity is not an option, and our children's natural honesty should not be compromised by sending them mixed messages. In short, children learn by example.

As a nation, we should make every attempt to elect honest politicians. Our children are becoming inundated with news about dishonest leaders who compromise integrity for popularity. It is no wonder that many of them are confused and frustrated. Their language is about "Keeping it Real"–they are not fooled. Let us remember that the future of our nation and its role in the world rests on our ability to gain the trust and respect of other nations. How can we do this is we do not first gain our children's? We must make every effort to communicate to young people that it is indeed essential to "keep it real" by dealing with them honestly and with integrity. Finally, we must send our children the clear message that it is more important to put principle over popularity if they hope to make a better world.

PROUD TO DISAGREE WITH INTEGRITY

Edson Mota, 11th Grade

In the race of life, I know that death will catch up to me before I even savor the experience. Therefore, I must begin to fulfill my sole purpose in life now, while applying the *Laws of Life* to help guide me along the way. The personal law of life that guides me most is integrity.

I used to think it was so cliché when adults would say, "Have some integrity." Yet, that was only because I didn't understand what they were trying to imply. Only when I was in high school did I fully understand it. Nowadays, I laugh at my foolishness because even though I did not quite understand the word integrity and the book definition, it was still something that I always had. In high school, I came to understand it through one of my classes. One of the first things that I learned in the JROTC drill team was the Air Force core values: "Integrity first, service before self, and excellence in all we do." Initially, I thought that this was just another thing we had to memorize, and I never stopped to think about what it meant. But, one day I just happened to open my workbook and came across the core values. This was a defining moment in my life.

I thought about the first one, integrity first, for a long time. I recall looking up the word to get clear on its meaning. The dictionary defined it as "a steadfast adherence to a strict moral or ethical code." Soon, I began to question my integrity, how true was I to my morals. What did I need to do to improve my sense of honor? This is when I began to change mentally.

I said I always had integrity because I've always had strict morals. For the most part I've always had a position on any topic, and it did not change drastically over the years. I knew myself and what I wanted. I also knew what I believed to be moral and immoral, and always followed this. However, when I read that statement, integrity first, I realized that recently I had not been adhering to my morals because I wasn't defending them. Often times in class someone would respond to a question, and I had a completely different point of view, yet I never felt it necessary to give my opinion. This is the part of me that was changed the most.

After I began to question my integrity, I began to change mentally. I now realized that I had an obligation to share my morals and ethics. My goal wasn't to convince people to think like me, but to just be unafraid to be that one person who isn't square, and to be proud of my principles. Since nobody else on this earth thinks like me it would be selfish of me to allow people to be one sided. This is when I realized my purpose in life.

I had always pondered my purpose on earth, yet I was not so driven to do this as I was to achieve success. My dream was of a grander life with an incredible amount of success and happiness, but I dreamed harder about a memorable and meaningful purpose in life. Certainly I would love to be the next Nelson Mandela, Ghandi, or Caesar Chavez, but I realize that may be asking too much. Therefore, I will settle for "plan c" to simply influence others to be more open-minded. Open-mindedness is the key to peace, and who doesn't want peace? I can help enlighten people by sharing my opinion and ethics. Yet I understand that they will have different options when they decide to stand for something. I noticed that a lot of people often think one-sidedly, but this is only because they don't know that another side exists. These people never put themselves in another person's position. As a result, I decided that I will try to open people's eyes to as much truth as I can. Integrity will help me fulfill my purpose in life because it will keep me focused, and make sure that whenever I hear an opinion that opposes mine I will say I disagree.

In conclusion, it is important to "have some integrity." It will help me fulfill my purpose of opening the minds of others and making sure I don't get lost along the way. My sense of integrity has allowed me to be proud of my individuality.

EULOGY: TRUTH

Anonymous, 8th Grade

Truth, what a known name in my life, and in the life of others as well. We have all noticed Truth's presence, until it disappeared. Why can't we all live forever? Truth has awarded us with the pure good of us knowing that we can be honest to ourselves and others. Now that Truth is gone, we have nothing but lies, no lessons to learn, nothing to earn. We are left with the flaws that lie deep beneath our skin, yet planted for us still deeper beneath the earth's core.

Truth, why did you have to leave us? Truth gives us the purity and the reality. I remember long ago when Truth and I were outside and we noticed that it was a nice day. Well it's a pretty long story so I am going to make things short. I got in trouble for knocking over my mother's vase. And, I had lied. Truth didn't talk to me, so I knew it was because of my lying to my mother. Truth wrote me a note about how I should be true to myself and honest to others and to do the right thing. So I then went to my mother and told her the truth–and got grounded for a month. Yet, I bet if I had told the truth the first time she would have given me a week. Truth talked to me and we were once again cool. Actually I did feel better that I told her. I thanked Truth because Truth was right and I was wrong for lying.

See what an influence Truth had on me? Not only on me, but also on others. Truth taught so many people how to be honest. Now that Truth is gone everything has crumbled. Crashed. Burned. Destroyed. OVER. Why did you leave? You have caused lots of peace, now very little remains alive. Goodness is very scarce. Now that Truth is gone, lies have taken us over and destroyed every ounce of respect that we have for one another. If Truth were here, everyone would know that we have to do what is right. We would know how to be honest. Honesty was Truth's number one policy as far as friends or family were concerned. It is very amazing how truth told us that the right way was the better way and that the grass is much greener on the other side.

Even though some of us enjoy its good influence, have knowledge and strength to be honest, others still don't know how to stay true. They stick with lying because that's what they breathe—a whole bunch of lies that will get them nowhere in life except into all different kinds of trouble. Truth left us after sharing with us its knowledge of what we should expect in life when we do good things. Truth told us that we get what we deserved. Like karma. When we do good, we get good things in return; if we are dedicated to the bad things we receive bad things. Truth has taught me to be a more careful judge of things and to therefore avoid the bad things that I used to engage in. It has touched all of our lives. Why was Truth's time so short on this earth? Truth's remains are very scarce. We find Truth's influence everywhere, in the souls of people and on places on earth. Truth left us a poem called "do right." Here it is:

> *Turn left and turn right,*
> *What do you see?*
> *You see me,*
> *Doing the right,*
> *yeah doing the right thing,*
> *I do right as you do wrong,*
> *you want me to fight,*
> *I just want to get along*
> *Why are you messing with?*
> *Telling me lies instead of the truth,*
> *Why are you fronting,*
> *Doing things you know you shouldn't do,*
> *Why act like a fool,*
> *Don't be that fool stay in school,*
> *Do the right not the wrong,*
> *Don't cry and wander,*
> *be cool and stay strong,*
> *You want to have fun,*
> *You want to fit in,*
> *Do right and win,*
> *You laugh in others' faces,*
> *You always think you're right.*
> *Back off from the fight,*
> *You think you're big and tough,*
> *You can punch out my lights,*
> *Yet don't be a loser,*
> *Win and "do right."*

Truth has many talents, and, as you can see, its words are full of much meaning. Don't throw these words of wisdom away. Stay focused on what Truth says. Truth has left this earth, yet we can still bring back its positive influence and get rid of all our negativity. Peace to Truth and to all. Amen.

YOU LOSE TRUST WHEN YOU LIE

Vidya Budhan, 8th Grade

People often believe they will not get in trouble for simple things. That is not always the case. Remember, it is always better to tell the truth than to tell a lie. Honesty plays a big role in each and everyone's life. Therefore, we must all be faithful to what is right. In the past, honesty didn't seem like a big issue. However, one small experience taught me a big lesson.

Recently, we had a half-a-day school session and I forgot to tell my mom. Instead of going home early, I decided to go hang out with my friend. We didn't do anything bad. We went to the local library to get some books to study for an upcoming test. I actually thought I was going to get away with this. I went home as though we had a full-day dismissal only to find out that nothing would be as I expected.

When I got home, there were two police cars in front of my house. I started to panic, running inside the house as fast as I could. I saw my mom talking to two police officers. When I said "What's going on?" my mom got up and said, "Oh, my God, Thank God you're safe!!!" My mom walked the policemen to the door, thanking them for their help. When she came back, we had a very long talk about this unforgettable experience.

The first thing she asked me was, "Where have you been all this time?" I responded with "school." She asked me the same question again and I responded with the same answer. My mom's worried face turned into a frown. I started to feel dizzy and hot at the same time. She asked me why I was lying to her. I didn't respond.

Then she told me that one of my friends called her asking for me and told my mom about the half-day session. I became very angry. I decided to tell her the truth. I said, "I was at the library" but of course, she didn't believe me. After that day, I lost my mom's trust.

That one little lie still caused so much pain. It still affects me. Every time I asked my mom to go somewhere, she looks at me strangely or with a grin. I have lost her trust. To this day, she does not believe I spent that day in the library. My mom asks me every month to bring home a monthly school agenda with all scheduled meetings, half-days, conferences, etc.–all because I have lost her trust.

Hopefully, my experience will persuade you to be honest about everything because we never know what humiliating, negative consequences can result from lying. Honesty is one of the most important *Laws of Life*.

TRUTH

Cleo Murphy-Guerette, 5th Grade

"The truth always matters." This is what my mom always said when she was not sure if I was telling the truth. I was so young that I never really cared, that is, until I met Gemma. Little did I know she would become a teacher to me as well as a friend.

I met Gemma in kindergarten and we immediately became good friends. She also told me that the truth matters. Of course, I never really listened to her either. She was just a friend who supposedly knew everything about everything, especially the truth. She supported me with trust, and I never realized how important she was to me, until she let me down by telling a lie herself.

It was a warm, sunny day in August, and I was sitting in Gemma's room waiting for her to stop pacing around. She said she had told a lie to her mom. She was ashamed of herself and afraid that she would never again trust her. I did not understand why this was so important. But then, she did something that amazed me. She went downstairs and told her mom that she had lied. That is when I got it. When she told her mom, it triggered something inside me that made me understand that the truth *does* matter. It really is important to tell the truth. We make decisions every day to do either the right or wrong thing. I also realized that telling the truth is one of the most important things we do. So if Gemma could face her fears, tell the truth *and* risk getting in trouble, so can I. Now, because of Gemma, I always try to tell the truth. It is always my first choice. So now, when I ever consider telling a lie, I just think of Gemma and how important it was to her to always tell the truth, and it reminds me that the best things to do in any situation is tell the truth. Even if you know you will be risking getting in trouble, you will be risking a lot more if you lie. You will be risking losing someone's trust.

Gemma moved away quite a long time ago, but I often think of her. We write letters sometimes and I miss her. But most of all I miss her truthfulness, because the truth always matters.

BEING HONEST IS BEST, BUT IT CAN BE HARD

Gary Pastuna, 5th Grade

One day something happen in my life that changed me: It made me become honest. This is how it started. I was walking from school and heard a dog. It was by a tree. It was a small puppy. I picked him up and took him home. He was afraid and cold.

While I was taking him home, I remembered that my mother didn't like dogs or cats. I was thinking of a way to tell my mom and dad. "That's it!" I thought to myself, "I can tell her that I will keep the dog in my room." I ran home to tell her.

When I got home, I begged her to keep him, telling her I was going to take care of him and leave him in my room. I told my father, too, and they went to their room to decide. I was really nervous. I drank 20 cups of water. When they finally came out I was sweating like I had just come out of the pool. They said I could keep the puppy. I was so happy. My mom said, "First you have to take him to the veterinarian to check if he is sick." I told my mom, "I love you." I ran to the vet. When I got to the veterinarian I asked the nurse if she could check the puppy she responded, "Sure." After she was done, I went home.

I had another appointment for him next week at 3:00. I told my mom he was O.K. and wasn't sick. I could only keep the puppy in my room. I decided to give him the name "Rick!" He liked the name. We decided to eat pizza. It tasted hot and soft. We walked home after we were done and I saw something amazing on the tree.

There was a picture of Rick with the word "Missing." I wondered if Rick was someone's puppy. I took the paper because there was a number. When I got home I got the phone and dialed the number. A little girl picked up and I asked her if she lost a puppy. She screamed out, "Yes! Yes!" I told her my address so she could come and get him. My mom heard the whole thing. She told me I was really honest.

The door bell rang. It was the little girl. Rick ran to the little girl and she thanked me. I saw the girl go across the street she yelled I could come over any day to visit. It was unbelievable.

I learned that honesty is always best. Sometimes it is difficult to do the right thing, but it is important to always tell the truth.

SAVED FROM THE SINKING SAND

Bryanna Shelton, 5th Grade

Have you ever heard someone say that they're in sinking sand? I have heard this said before, several times. You probably have too, but maybe not in these exact words. The phrase, "I'm in sinking sand" refers to the fact there's a problem. You are trying to solve it, but no matter what you do, you just keep falling deeper and deeper into it. The story that I am about to tell is about two of my friends who experienced this.

Alex and Alicia are my two older friends. They are eleven-year-old twin sisters who are in a gang. They are both in the sixth grade. They are really smart, but they don't use their brains like they should. Every day I would see them, I would try to talk them out of the "gang stuff."

One day, Alex and Alicia's gang buddies dared them to steal money from a local convenience store. So that night, they attempted to rob the Quick Check down the street from my house. In the process of doing so, they injured the storeowner by beating him with the ice cream from the freezer in the front of the store and then growing hot coffee at him. They felt bad about what they had done. Their conscience bothered them so much that they decided to sneak over to my house to talk to me about what had happened. After listening to what they had to say, I just told them they were stuck in a deep hole. I let them know that it was getting too deep for them to get out of on their own. I also told them that if they didn't get out of it, something really bad was going to happen to them.

I told them they needed to go to the police and tell them everything. After giving them my perspective on the situation, I had prayer with them. Then I quoted the words of a song I remembered by Grandmother singing called, "On Christ the Solid Rock I stand." The part of the song that I wanted them to understand was: "On Christ the solid rock I stand, all other ground is sinking sand, all other ground is sinking sand." I also told them that if they would confess their sins and tell the truth, then they would be free emotionally. I told them that they did a terrible thing and that they would be punished for it, but they needed to take responsibility for their actions. After listening and talking together, they left my home.

Several days went by and I did not see nor hear from them. However, when I picked up the newspaper, guess what I read? In the local section, there was an article about a Quick Check owner and a set of twin girls who had robbed him. It stated that they had gone back to the store to apologize to the owner and to return the money, but also that the girls had been sentenced to serve two years in a juvenile delinquency program. Police officers involved in the investigation were surprised to have the two "perpetrators" return to the scene of the crime, turn themselves in and say, "I'm sorry."

Two years later, Alex and Alicia were released from jail. During their time there they had realized that life in a gang was tough and dangerous. They had also realized that stealing was wrong, whereas before they felt that people who had a lot of stuff could afford to be "ripped-off." They learned that they had to be responsible for their actions and that there were consequences for their behavior. Also, they learned that the *Laws of Life* are not just about obeying the rules, but also doing the right thing. And, they now know that honesty is the best policy. If you're honest you don't have to worry about getting the story right, because you've already told it right. They learned the importance of integrity, of doing what's right all the time. The twins also got a better understanding of "good citizenship," getting along with other people. Most of all, they learned the importance of making good decisions and being responsible for them.

Now that you have heard this story, I hope that you will remember that there's no need to "sink in the sand." Faith in God and the *Laws of Life* can help you through any situation.

Appendix for Educators

HOW AND WHY TO CARRY OUT
LAWS OF LIFE WRITING ACTIVITIES

Part One: The Connection between the Laws of Life, Character Education, and Literacy

Sir John Templeton, and another social philanthropist, John Fetzer, shared a profound insight: There is much in the unseen world of heart and soul that would bring great benefit to humanity if we knew how to tap into it. The *Laws of Life* essays, and related formats that we have developed, do exactly that. We invite educators to enter this world and begin to derive from it the many benefits it offers–for yourself and then, through your actions, for the children who will take over leadership roles in our world as they move into adulthood. It is essential that they be prepared with both literacy skills and sound character.

In 2001, a seminal article in *Education Week* entitled, "What's Wrong and What's Right with Character Education" laid the groundwork for the *Laws of Life* essay. The authors pointed out that the pedagogy of many approaches to character education was weak in light of the strong competing messages students receive to behave in ways that are more impulsive and expedient, and less thoughtful than those who care deeply about children would desire them to be. Recent studies have expanded our understanding of the social-emotional benefits that flow from the proper expression of one's emotions, concerns, and plans.

This, of course, parallels considerable research into compliance with various therapeutic activities in health fields and our knowledge of the power of ongoing testimonials in alcoholism recovery. Our own research suggests that there are benefits to students who write *Laws of Life* essays; beyond that, expressing their *Laws of Life* in a personally salient way allows them to more successfully identify their own laws, become aware of them, elaborate them, and apply them in various life situations.

Because the *Laws of Life* essays are so meaningful to students, they enjoy writing them and are willing to accept feedback and improve on them. They contain sentiments and experiences that students want to convey to others. In addition to generally working on literacy, students are genuinely interested in hearing about one-another's *Laws of Life*. They are therefore willing to give and get feedback and further expand their literacy skills as part of being in a caring, learning community of character.

Part Two: Elements of a Laws of Life Essay:

Guidelines for Introducing it into Existing Literacy Curricula and Assignments

A *Laws of Life* essay can be introduced in a language arts class in grades five and up. There are a wide variety of formats and approaches, but an outline of the most typical way educators can help students generate essays is given below. The reader should note that the various steps in the process have been used in different sequences and are sometimes combined, etc. Circumstances will determine how to best use these guidelines. Following them allows one to score the essay. It also provides students with feedback for improving their *Laws of Life* essays and their overall written communication.

1. Identify "Laws of Life" and show where they can be found.

Present the idea of a *Law of Life* to students. Typically, they understand the *Laws of Life* as a rule or set of rules, or a saying that expresses the way we want to live. Another way to think about a *Law of Life* is as a kind of summary of how someone has lived. We usually do this after the fact, oftentimes even after someone has passed away. You might want to bring up figures your students have read about or discussed in fiction or history and have them try to summarize a given law or a number of *Laws of Life* that capture the achievement of such an historic figure. Build toward the idea that every day, we are writing our *Laws of Life* by the choices we make about how we conduct ourselves. The *Laws of Life* can be found everywhere. They are evident in what people say and do, and we see them when we look back at people's lives, their choices and actions. The assignment you are going to give students is to help them think about, express, and share their current law or *Laws of Life* -the ideas, values, principles, virtues, etc. that guide them through every day.

2. *Provide writing prompts.*

Writing prompts help students start thinking. They also serve as a bridge from the concept of *Laws of Life* to students' beginning to identify their own. Many different prompts can be used (depending on students' age and the context of the writing assignment). There are, however, some that we have proven most effective. Some teachers find it useful to have each student write their answer to some or all of the prompts. Also, teachers sometimes have students share these in pairs prior with a segment of a class class. In other cases, they have encouraged sharing with the entire class. In every case, teachers try to follow up students' statements by helping them think more deeply about their answers (e.g., What makes these qualities worth admiring, copying? How did you choose that particular incident or example or person? Why are these qualities, values so important to you?)

- Whom do you admire? List three of that person's admirable qualities.
- Describe an incident or event from which you learned a lesson "the hard way."
- What could you change about yourself to become a better person?
- What three qualities do you value in a friend? A teacher? A parent?
- Who has been most important in your life in helping you establish your values? Explain.
- When you become a parent, what are the three most important values that you hope to instill in your children?

3. *Share the Laws of Life that students write about.*

After students have had a chance to think about the prompts and perhaps jot down some initial thoughts, have a group discussion about those *Laws of Life* that students have pondered and selected. This does not mean they have made a final choice. Some students might even share several that they are considering. However, it can be useful for them to get a sense of what their classmates are thinking about. It also plants valuable seeds as regards the process of the deeper sharing that will be done when their written drafts are complete.

4. *Provide guidelines for the specific writing assignment of the essay.*

Laws of Life writing assignments can take the form of narrative or factual essays, play dialogues, shorter or longer forms of stories from everyday life, or even fiction. The requirement that certain grammatical forms must be used can might provide useful and instructive constraints on the writing process. There are many ways to convey one's *Laws of Life* and students will no doubt be better at some forms than others. But all of them should be able to be connected to work that is done in other areas of the existing curriculum and other assignments. (NOTE: Sometimes this step comes earlier. It can frame the overall assignment and can be introduced earlier in a general way, then elaborated in greater detail.)

5. Discuss the basis upon which students are drawing as they write about their Law of Life.

As students start to think about their writing, it is helpful to ask them what they are going to draw from as they think about their *Law of Life*. Having them listen to one another's ideas before they start writing often helps spark deeper reflections. Some examples are as follows:

* a personal role model (grandparent, parents, sibling, other relative, teacher, member of the clergy, coach, etc.)
* a figure in contemporary life or history
* someone whose life they read about in a book, article, story
* a quote, maxim, proverb, section of scripture
* a story, myth, legend, or fable
* an important life experience they had or heard about that has influenced their life since (it can be a positive or negative example, i.e., how to be or how NOT to be)

6. Provide guidelines and opportunities for small group peer editing and feedback.

Depending on the specific curriculum area or assignment, provide guidance to peer groups and allow children in groups of three or four to share and comment on each other's writing. Some or all of the items below may prove helpful, perhaps in addition to your own specific guidelines. This rubric has been used effectively by students in Grades 8 and above.

7. Give student summary feedback and parameters for revision.

Confer with each student, help him or her sort out the feedback they have received, provide your own, and help them leave with a plan for making revisions.

8. Arrange for essays to be shared with parents, guardians, family.

Bringing a family member into a conversation about character is very important. Arrange a suitable time and way for students to share their essays with those at home. Sensitivity to individual family circumstances is, of course, important as well.

9. Final feedback and editing process.

Provide a deadline and process for creating the final version of the work. In some cases, it will be submitted as a class assignment. In others, there will be the opportunity to post the students' work on classroom or hallway walls or a bulletin board. Sometimes written work is gathered into a notebook or folder and kept in the classroom so students can read others' essays when they like. This promotes classroom cohesion and awareness of others. Of course, if the written works will be part of a *Laws of Life* contest, then a procedure for selecting/submitting them should be followed from this point onward.

Part Three: A Rubric for Evaluating Laws of Life Essays

A unique rubric for scoring and evaluating *Laws of Life* essays was created by the *Laws of Life* team in Plainfield, New Jersey. It emphasizes the social and emotional content, e.g. the importance and value of the message, the conviction of the writer, and the uniqueness of the story. The rubric is intended for use by student screeners, judges and adult community judges. Student screeners and judges participated in a training program to help them gain familiarity with it. This program included discussions of their opinions of sample essays with their fellow evaluators. The students were instructed to use the rubric as well as to "follow their heart" when scoring the essays. Generally, each essay is scored by two individuals. Scores can be averaged; where there are significant discrepancies in evaluation, a conference between scorers usually results in a consensus rating.

In addition to its applicability in the context of a *Laws of Life* contest, the rubric can also be used, in whole or in part, in other classroom writing assignments. For example, when an assignment is focused on helping students develop their sense of voice, the one designed for this topic can be applied.

For each of the 5 topic areas, essays are rated along a 4 point scale:

WOW!!! (4)
YES! (3)
OK (2)
???? (1)

The definition of each of these respective to topics is provided below. Considerations are made for the grade level of the child and specific requirements of the language arts instructional approaches being used in their schools. Typically, the ratings are arranged in a format that teachers, screeners, and judges (whether they are students' colleagues or community members) find easy to use.

TOPIC: CONTENT
The heart of the message.
Does the essay focus on a law that would make the world a better place if everyone practiced it? Would most people agree it is an important one?

(4) The topic captures the essence of a law. The author demonstrates full understanding of what a law of life is and writes about it from his/her heart.
(3) The topic is an appropriate law of life. The author shows an adequate understanding of what a law of life is and writes from a personal perspective, but not necessarily from his/her heart.
(2) The topic would not necessarily be considered a law of life by most people. The author shows some understanding of what such a law is and writes about it in a slightly personal and/or emotional way.
(1) The topic is inappropriate as a law of life. The author does not seem to understand what such a law is. The essay is not written from a personal or emotional perspective.

TOPIC: VOICE

The feelings and convictions of the writer are expressed.
Did the essay make you both think and feel? Did you feel drawn into it? Did you learn something special about the author?
(4) The personality of the writer is clear, and, upon reading the essay, the reader feels as if he and the writer were having a personal conversation. The writer is unafraid to boldly and honestly state his/her opinions and feelings. The essay is engaging.
(3) The personality of the writer comes across but on a superficial level, as if he/she is in a casual conversation. The writer simply states his/her opinions and feelings. The tone of the essay is enjoyable and earnest, but not necessarily engaging.
(2) The personality of the writer comes out only once in a while. The writer does not often give his/her opinions or feelings and tends to use safe generalizations. The tone of the essay is pleasant but businesslike. The reader is not fully engaged.
(a) The writer seems distant and his/her personality does not come out. The writer's statements seem to hide his or her true feelings about the topic. The tone of the essay is unpleasant (e.g. monotone) and does not engage the reader.

TOPIC: UNIQUENESS

Distinctiveness of the ideas and presentation.
Does the essay capture a value or an ideal in a unique and special way? Is it interestingly and creatively written?
(4) The author presents a fresh, compelling, and creative view on an important value.
(3) The author presents a fresh and fairly creative view on a value.
(2) The author's perspective is only slightly unique and creative.

(1)   The author's perspective is unoriginal and unimaginative.

TOPIC: ORGANIZATION

The internal structure and pattern of ideas.

Is the essay easy to read? Is it clearly written? Were you able to tell exactly what the author was trying to share? Do the ideas and paragraphs flow smoothly?

(4)   The essay is well organized. The main idea is clear and the essay flows smoothly. The reader never feels lost or confused.

(3)   The essay is generally organized. The main idea is highlighted, but the essay doesn't flow perfectly smoothly.

(2)   The essay shows some organization. The structure moves the reader without too much confusion and sometimes supports the main idea.

(1)   The essay lacks organization and is confusing. It is hard for the reader to get a grip on the main point, and a clear sense of direction is lacking.

MECHANICS

Correctness of writing.

Is this a publishable piece or are there grammar and spelling mistakes?

(4)   No spelling and grammar errors.

(3)   A few spelling and grammar errors that affect meaning.

(2)   Some spelling and grammar errors that make meaning unclear.

(1)   Many spelling and grammar errors that make meaning unclear.